# SEVEN SEAS' GHOST SHIP PRESENTS

# WORL...
# HA...

### art by KOTARO SH...

MW00577798

TRANSLATION
Ben Trethewey

ADAPTATION
Sam Mitchell

LETTERING AND LAYOUT
mono

COVER DESIGN
Nicky Lim

PROOFREADER
Dawn Davis

EDITOR
Elise Kelsey

PREPRESS TECHNICIAN
Rhiannon Rasmussen-Silverstein

PRODUCTION MANAGER
tillo, George Panella (Ghost Ship)

MANAGING EDITOR
Julie Davis

ASSOCIATE PUBLISHER
Adam Arnold

PUBLISHER
Jason DeAngelis

Seven Seas press and purchase enquiries can be sent to Marketing Manager
Lianne Sentar at press@gomanga.com. Information regarding the distribution
and purchase of digital editions is available from Digital Manager CK Russell
at digital@gomanga.com.

Seven Seas, Ghost Ship, and their accompanying logos are trademarks of
Seven Seas Entertainment. All rights reserved.

ISBN: 978-1-64827-506-7

Printed in Canada

First Printing: October 2021

10 9 8 7 6 5 4 3 2 1

## FOLLOW US ONLINE: www.ghostshipmanga.com

# READING DIRECTIONS

This book reads from *right to left*, Japanese style.
If this is your first time reading manga, you start
reading from the top right panel on each page and
take it from there. If you get lost, just follow the
numbered diagram here. It may seem backwards at
first, but you'll get the hang of it! Have fun!!

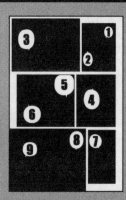

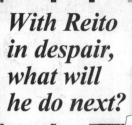

*With Reito in despair, what will he do next?*

Hello everyone.

My name is Doi Shota.

I WANT TO BE ALONE.

*Shota and Karen make moves to consolidate their power.*

*A new crisis threatens the world!*

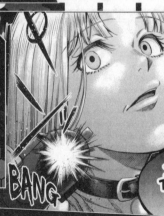

BANG

I DID SOMETHING TO THE VACCINE.

# WORLD'S END HAREM Part Two Coming Soon!!

# Afterword

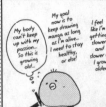

My body can't keep up with my passion... So this is growing old...

My goal now is to keep drawing manga as long as I'm alive... I need to stay healthy, or else!

I feel like I'm getting slower and slower as I grow older.

This has been my first long-running serialization, yet here we are with an anime adaption! I can keep writing to my heart's content... Thank you.

I hope in these past four years I've been able to grow, even a little, as a mangaka...

Turns out I don't actually have that much to say, now that I think about it.

Thank you so much for buying volume twelve of *World's End Harem*! I'm so grateful to all of you for continuing to read this far... Next up, part two of the story!

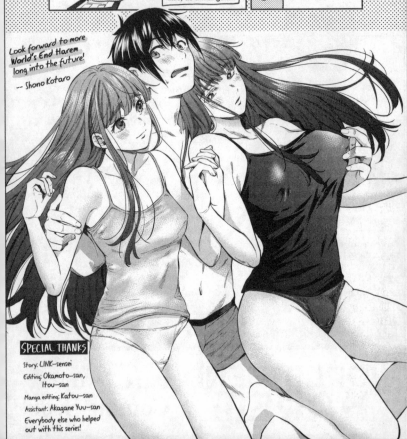

Look forward to more *World's End Harem* long into the future!
-- Shono Kotaro

## SPECIAL THANKS

Story: LINK-sensei

Editing: Okamoto-san, Itou-san

Manga editing: Katou-san

Assistant: Akagane Yuu-san

Everybody else who helped out with this series!

# Afterword

## Part One – Author's Note

It has now been almost four years since this project began, and roughly five since I approached Shono-sensei with the idea of a manga adaption. In that time so much has happened around the world, and personally to me on a smaller scale. When I think back to when serialization first started, I remember "back then nobody was worried about the coronavirus," "everybody in Japan was looking forward to the Olympics," and "We managed to get *World's End Harem* back on iOS." Right now, I feel like Reito must've felt waking up from cryosleep, thinking about how much the world has changed...

The story isn't over yet, so I'm not going to get too caught up in reminiscing. Most of all, I'd like to give all the gratitude I possibly can to Shono-sensei. Thank you for sending me all your amazing first drafts. Let's go get some food again once all this calms down!

Next, to all the editorial staff at *Shonen Jump+*, and all the different editors we've had over the years. Thank you for taking a risk in serializing this work. Without your continued support and encouragement, this manga wouldn't be the boundary-breaking story it is today. You're all holy sex warriors, fighting for freedom of expression against the repressive forces of self-righteous moral outrage and intolerance. Let us go into battle together.

But since we're going to have to tackle them head on, I want to wrest the apple of victory from their grasp through wisdom and wit... That apple that started this all, the forbidden fruit Adam tasted in the Garden of Eden.

Thank you again to all those who have supported this work in paper, digital versions, and now even the anime staff. I look forward to continuing to work with you in the future.

Lastly, to my readers. I figured before I started writing that a lot of people were going to get *really* mad at me, but it's truly only because of your unexpected and continued support that this work is still in print. I'm sure parts of the story have gotten somewhat complicated at times. I've always intended to make the story interesting, not just a vehicle for lewdness and sex. In the upcoming part two we're really going back to the *World's End Harem* basics you've all come to expect. We're gonna have a harem! A harem!!!!! Reito, Shota, and the others will be back, of course. I hope you look forward to seeing everyone again soon. Well then, that's all!

July 2020, LINK

World's End Harem, Volume 12 (End)
Part One – END.

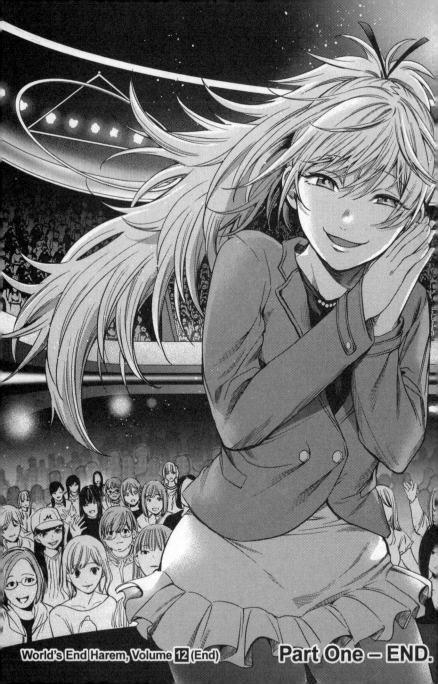

WHO DO YOU WANT TO HAVE FIRST?

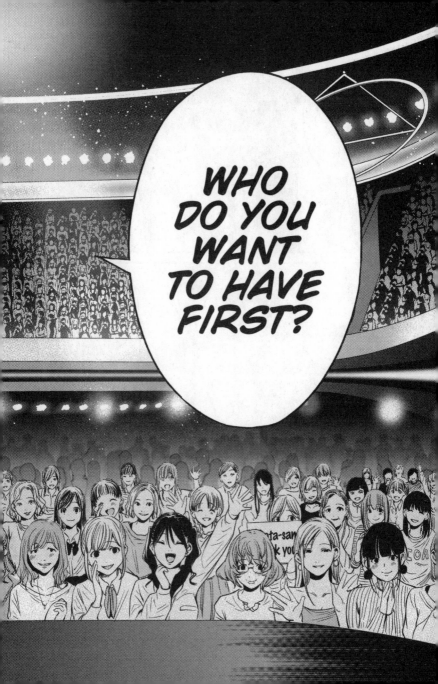

YOUR HAREM DOESN'T STOP HERE, SHOTA-SAMA, NOT BY A LONG SHOT!
ALL THE WOMEN IN JAPAN...
NO, I'LL GIVE YOU ALL THE WOMEN IN THE WORLD!
AND YOU'LL BE RIGHT THERE NEXT TO ME, ACTUALLY CALLING THE SHOTS.
Grin
WELL THEN...

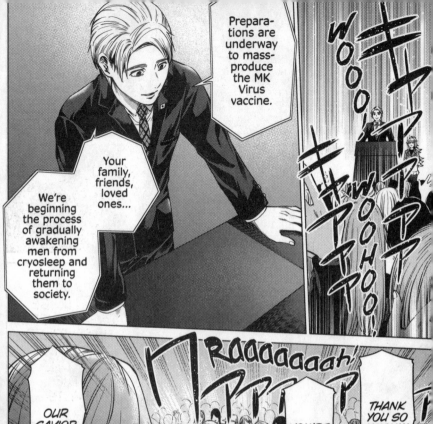

Preparations are underway to mass-produce the MK Virus vaccine.

Your family, friends, loved ones...

We're beginning the process of gradually awakening men from cryosleep and returning them to society.

WOOOO!

WHOHOO

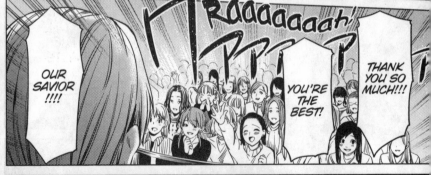

Raaaaaaah!

OUR SAVIOR !!!!

YOU'RE THE BEST!

THANK YOU SO MUCH!!!

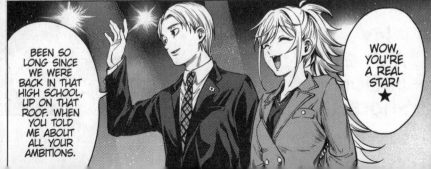

BEEN SO LONG SINCE WE WERE BACK IN THAT HIGH SCHOOL, UP ON THAT ROOF. WHEN YOU TOLD ME ABOUT ALL YOUR AMBITIONS.

WOW, YOU'RE A REAL STAR! ★

Woooo!
Chatter Chatter
Woohoo!
Chatter
DOI-SAAA-AAN!
SHOTA-SAN!
SHOTA-SAMA-AAA!!
Hello every-one.
My name is Doi Shota.

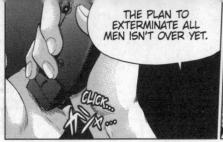

THE PLAN TO EXTERMINATE ALL MEN ISN'T OVER YET.

CLICK...

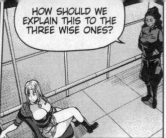

HOW SHOULD WE EXPLAIN THIS TO THE THREE WISE ONES?

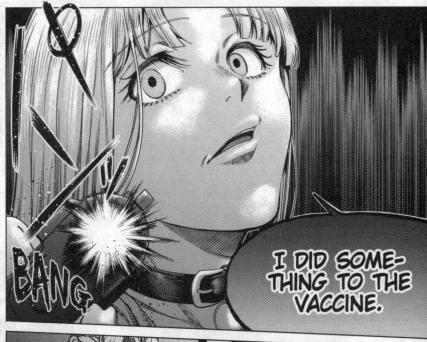

BANG

I DID SOMETHING TO THE VACCINE.

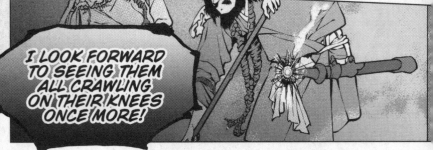

I LOOK FORWARD TO SEEING THEM ALL CRAWLING ON THEIR KNEES ONCE MORE!

BANG
BANG
BANG
BANG
BANG
..........
BANG

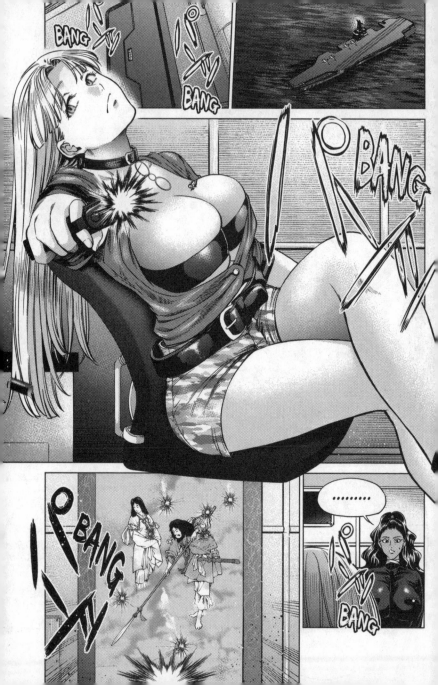

IT'S OKAY.
WE'VE ALREADY TALKED ABOUT THIS, HAVEN'T WE?
YOU AND I ARE ONE PERSON IN TWO BODIES.
THIS IS WHAT REITO NEEDS.

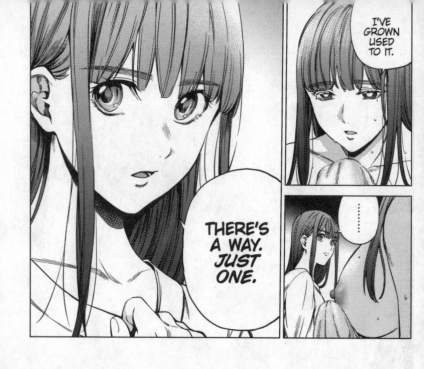

I'VE GROWN USED TO IT.

......

THERE'S A WAY. JUST ONE.

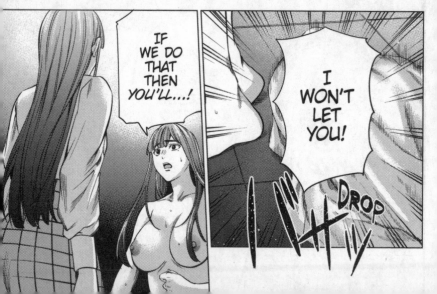

IF WE DO THAT THEN YOU'LL...!

I WON'T LET YOU!

DROP

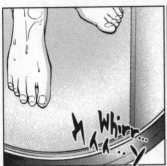

Whirr...

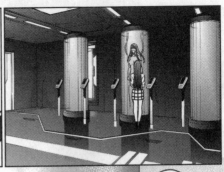

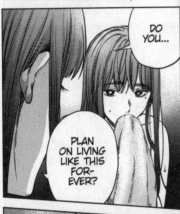

DO YOU...

PLAN ON LIVING LIKE THIS FOR-EVER?

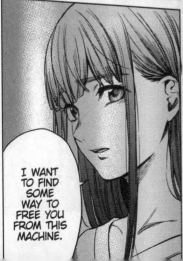

I WANT TO FIND SOME WAY TO FREE YOU FROM THIS MACHINE.

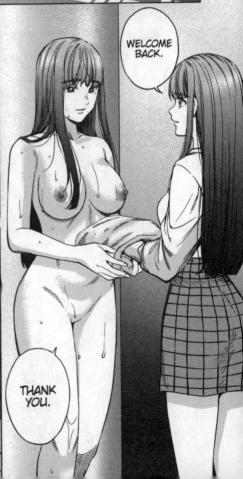

WELCOME BACK.

THANK YOU.

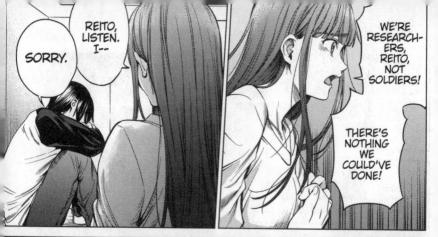

SORRY.

REITO, LISTEN. I--

WE'RE RESEARCH- ERS, REITO, NOT SOLDIERS!

THERE'S NOTHING WE COULD'VE DONE!

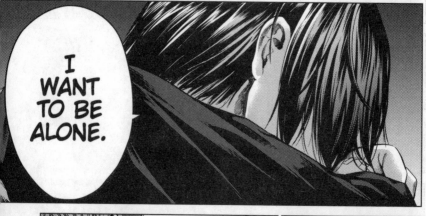

I WANT TO BE ALONE.

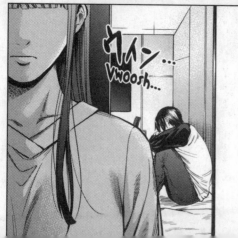

ヴィン... VWOOSH...

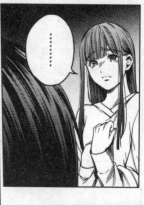

......

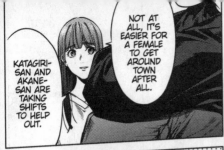

NOT AT ALL, IT'S EASIER FOR A FEMALE TO GET AROUND TOWN AFTER ALL.
KATAGIRI-SAN AND AKANE-SAN ARE TAKING SHIFTS TO HELP OUT.
I'M SORRY.
I DIDN'T MEAN FOR YOU TO HAVE TO CARE FOR KYOICHI-KUN AND YUKARI-SAN.
BABIES ARE SO CUTE, AREN'T THEY!
......
......
Silence...
IF ONLY...
I WERE STRONGER. I WOULD'VE BEEN ABLE TO SAVE HIM...

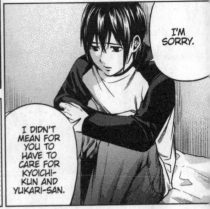

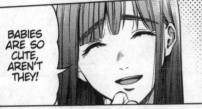

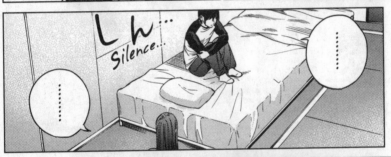

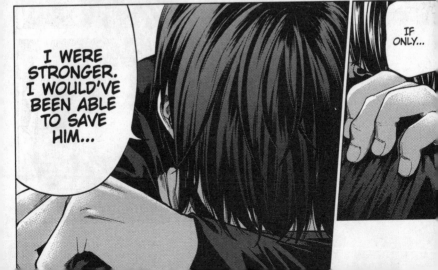

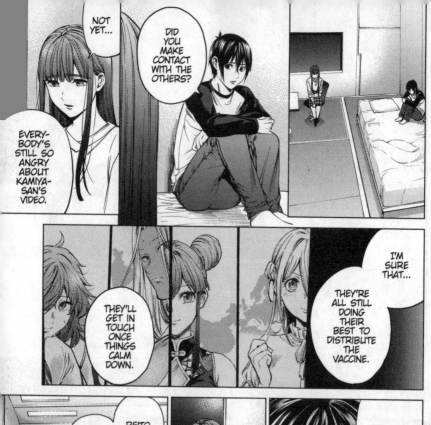

NOT YET...

DID YOU MAKE CONTACT WITH THE OTHERS?

EVERY-BODY'S STILL SO ANGRY ABOUT KAMIYA-SAN'S VIDEO.

THEY'LL GET IN TOUCH ONCE THINGS CALM DOWN.

I'M SURE THAT...

THEY'RE ALL STILL DOING THEIR BEST TO DISTRIBUTE THE VACCINE.

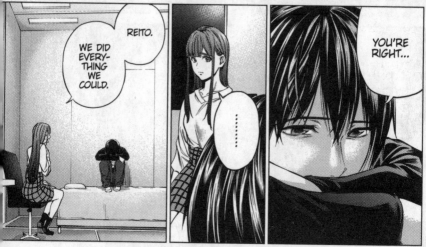

REITO.

WE DID EVERY-THING WE COULD.

‥‥‥‥‥

YOU'RE RIGHT...

IS MIZUHARA-SAN FINE WITH THE WAY THINGS STAND?
YEAH!
AFTER PATIENT TWO DIED HE'S BEEN *REEEAL* MOPEY, THOUGH!
I SUPPOSE THAT'S NOT TECHNICALLY A LIE EITHER.
I SEE...
HE'S SMART, BUT... TURNS OUT HIS MIND IS MORE FRAGILE THAN I THOUGHT.
CRASH

SO WE USE THE SLEEPING MEN AS BAIT TO BRING IN WOMEN! ★
I SHOULD'VE KNOWN YOU COULD DO IT!
NOTHING LIKE THE WAY UW TRIED TO PULL THIS OFF!
!
AH, I HAVE AN IDEA!
LET'S RELEASE YOUR IDENTITY TO THE CITIZENS...
IN A REAL THEATRICAL WAY, Y'KNOW?
WE TELL THEM YOU TOOK THE VACCINE DEVEL-OPED IN LOSANIA...
AND FOUND A WAY TO MASS-PRODUCE IT.
THAT'S HOW WE'LL ANNOUNCE IT!
YOU'LL BE WAY MORE POPULAR THAN PATIENT TWO IN NO TIME, SHOTA-SAMA!
LIKE, REALLY! ★
ぱっ
peace!

HOW MANY CRYO-SLEEP PODS ARE THERE HERE ANYWAY?
FIFTY THOUSAND?
A HUNDRED THOUSAND?
Mmh!
THAT SOUNDS ABOUT RIGHT TO ME!
THERE ARE OVER FIFTY MILLION WOMEN IN THE COUNTRY, RIGHT?
THE NUMBER THAT I CAN MATE WITH IS LIMITED.
WOMEN ARE GOING TO BECOME FRUSTRATED THAT MEN EXIST IF WE HOLD OUT ON THEM.
WE SHOULD MANAGE WHICH MALES WE THAW OUT...
AND CONDITION THEIR RELEASE ON THE CONTINUED COOPERATION OF THE FEMALES WE PROVIDE THEM TO.
THAT SHOULD GET US ONE STEP CLOSER TO YOUR GOAL, SHOULDN'T IT?

I REALLY LOVE YOU TOO, SHOTA-SAMA! ★
I'M HONORED.
SO...
WHAT'CHA WANNA DO ABOUT THE DRUGS?
I NEVER THOUGHT THEY'D REALLY SUCCEED IN MAKING A VACCINE.
MIZUHARA-SAN'S REALLY SOMETHING.
I'M SURE HERE IN JAPAN THERE'LL BE ENOUGH TO GO AROUND, BUT...
SHOULD WE CRUSH THEM?
I'VE GIVEN IT A LOT OF THOUGHT...
AND I THINK WE SHOULD WAKE AS MANY MALES AS POSSIBLE FROM CRYO-SLEEP.
WHAT MAKES YOU SAY THAT?

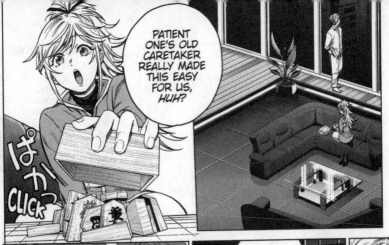

PATIENT ONE'S OLD CARETAKER REALLY MADE THIS EASY FOR US, *HUH*?

ぱか

CLICK

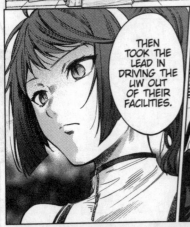

THEN TOOK THE LEAD IN DRIVING THE UW OUT OF THEIR FACILITIES.

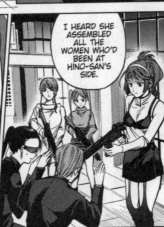

I HEARD SHE ASSEMBLED ALL THE WOMEN WHO'D BEEN AT HINO-SAN'S SIDE.

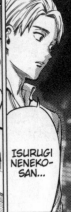

ISURUGI NENEKO-SAN...

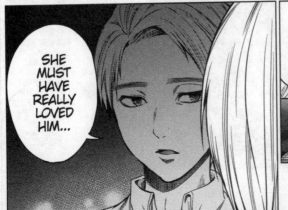

SHE MUST HAVE REALLY LOVED HIM...

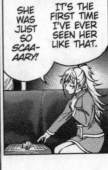

SHE WAS JUST SO SCAA-AARY!

IT'S THE FIRST TIME I'VE EVER SEEN HER LIKE THAT.

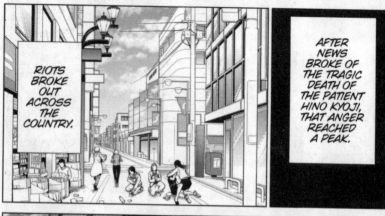

RIOTS BROKE OUT ACROSS THE COUNTRY.

AFTER NEWS BROKE OF THE TRAGIC DEATH OF THE PATIENT HINO KYOJI, THAT ANGER REACHED A PEAK.

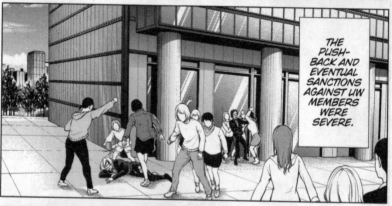

THE PUSH-BACK AND EVENTUAL SANCTIONS AGAINST UW MEMBERS WERE SEVERE.

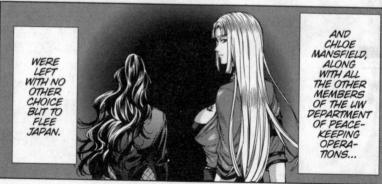

WERE LEFT WITH NO OTHER CHOICE BUT TO FLEE JAPAN.

AND CHLOE MANSFIELD, ALONG WITH ALL THE OTHER MEMBERS OF THE UW DEPARTMENT OF PEACE-KEEPING OPERA-TIONS...

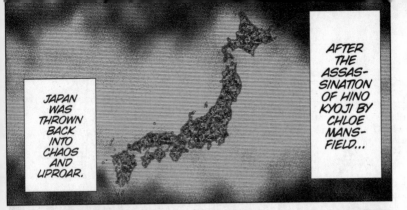

AFTER THE ASSAS-SINATION OF HINO KYOJI BY CHLOE MANS-FIELD...

JAPAN WAS THROWN BACK INTO CHAOS AND UPROAR.

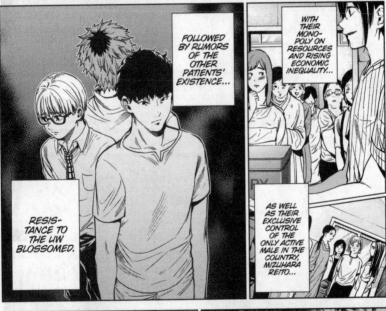

FOLLOWED BY RUMORS OF THE OTHER PATIENTS' EXISTENCE...

WITH THEIR MONO-POLY ON RESOURCES AND RISING ECONOMIC INEQUALITY...

RESIS-TANCE TO THE UW BLOSSOMED.

AS WELL AS THEIR EXCLUSIVE CONTROL OF THE ONLY ACTIVE MALE IN THE COUNTRY, MIZUHARA REITO...

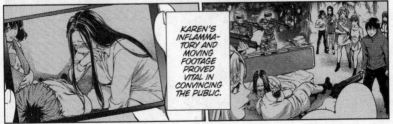

KAREN'S INFLAMMA-TORY AND MOVING FOOTAGE PROVED VITAL IN CONVINCING THE PUBLIC.

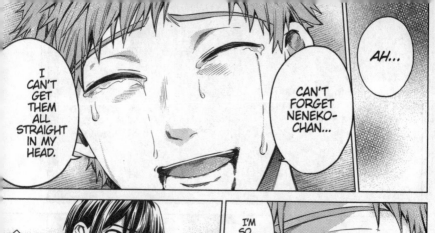

AH...

I CAN'T GET THEM ALL STRAIGHT IN MY HEAD.

CAN'T FORGET NENEKO-CHAN...

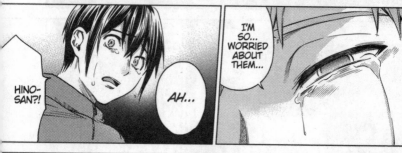

HINO-SAN?!

AH...

I'M SO... WORRIED ABOUT THEM...

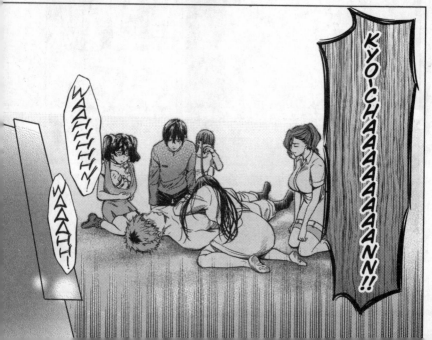

WAAAHH!

WAAAH!

KYO-CHAAAAANN!!

LOOK AFTER THEM FOR ME, WILL YOU?
YUKARI AND THE KID...
OF COURSE I WILL.
YOU FOCUS ON GETTING ALL HEALED UP...
AND GET BACK TO MAKING MORE KIDS, OKAY?
YOU'RE RIGHT...
RYOKO... KAEDE... SACHI-SAN... HONOKA...
RURI... NATSUMI... MAKIKO... SARA... SATOMI...
MAYA-CHAN... RENA... RIKA-SENPAI... KAORU...
MEGUMI... THE *OTHER* MEGUMI...

OUR FIRST BOY TOGETHER...
HE'S GOING TO BUILD THE FUTURE FOR US...
WHAT DO YOU THINK?
KYOICHI...
MIZU-HARA-KUN...
YOU THERE?
I'M HERE.
I WISH...
WE COULD'VE HAD...
MORE TIME TOGETHER. ALL THREE OF US.

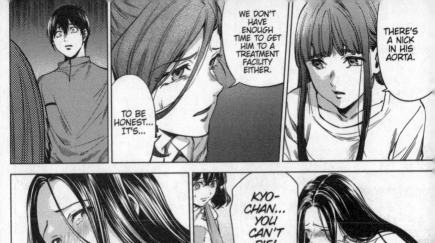

WE DON'T HAVE ENOUGH TIME TO GET HIM TO A TREATMENT FACILITY EITHER.

TO BE HONEST... IT'S...

THERE'S A NICK IN HIS AORTA.

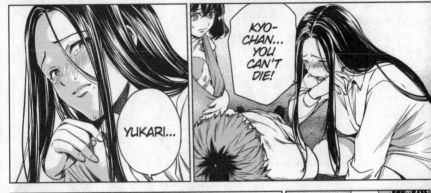

YUKARI...

KYO-CHAN... YOU CAN'T DIE!

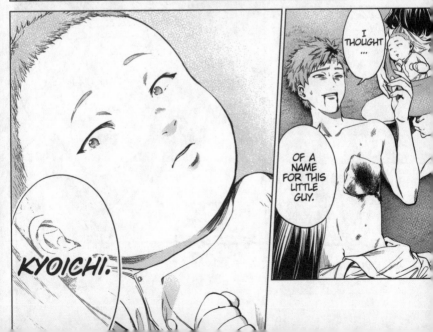

KYOICHI.

I THOUGHT...

OF A NAME FOR THIS LITTLE GUY.

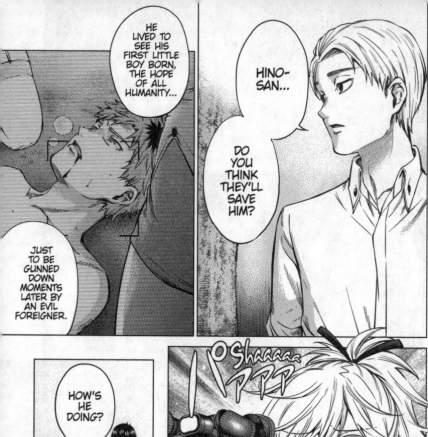

HE LIVED TO SEE HIS FIRST LITTLE BOY BORN, THE HOPE OF ALL HUMANITY...

HINO-SAN...

DO YOU THINK THEY'LL SAVE HIM?

JUST TO BE GUNNED DOWN MOMENTS LATER BY AN EVIL FOREIGNER.

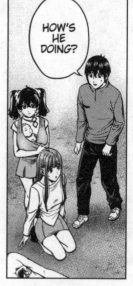

HOW'S HE DOING?

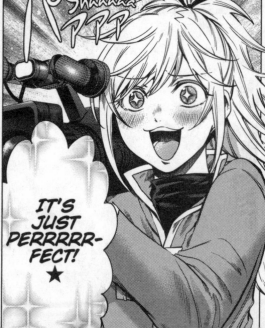

Shaaaaa PPP

IT'S JUST PERRRRR-FECT! ★

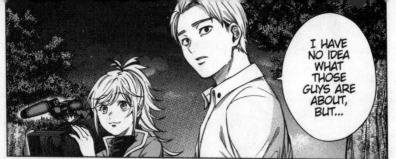

I HAVE NO IDEA WHAT THOSE GUYS ARE ABOUT, BUT...

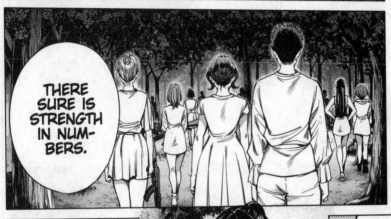

THERE SURE IS STRENGTH IN NUMBERS.

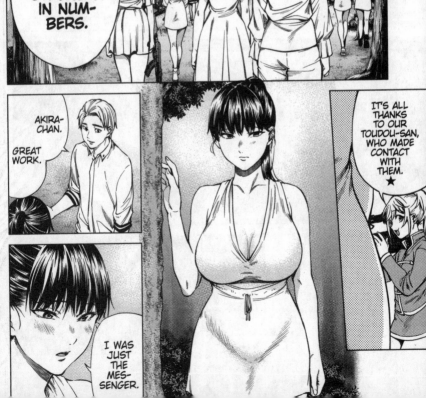

AKIRA-CHAN.

GREAT WORK.

IT'S ALL THANKS TO OUR TOUDOU-SAN, WHO MADE CONTACT WITH THEM. ★

I WAS JUST THE MESSENGER.

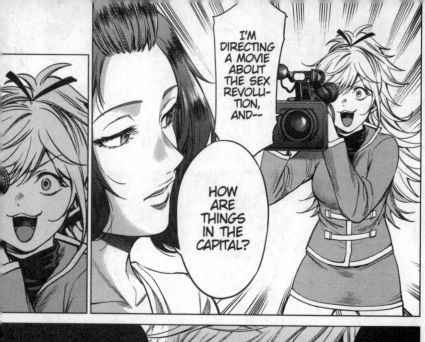

I'M DIRECTING A MOVIE ABOUT THE SEX REVOLUTION, AND--

HOW ARE THINGS IN THE CAPITAL?

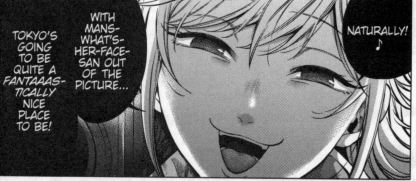

TOKYO'S GOING TO BE QUITE A FANTAAAASTICALLY NICE PLACE TO BE!

WITH MANS-WHAT'S-HER-FACE-SAN OUT OF THE PICTURE...

NATURALLY! ♪

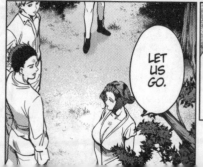

LET US GO.

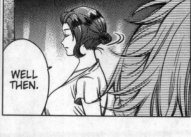

WELL THEN.

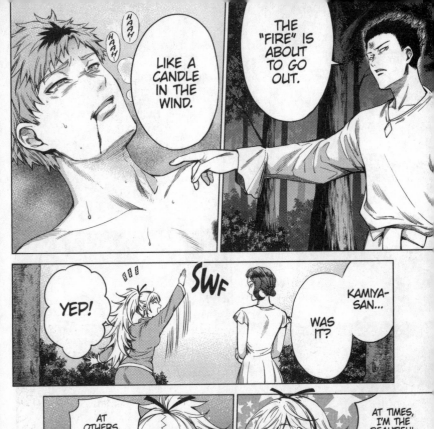

THE "FIRE" IS ABOUT TO GO OUT.

LIKE A CANDLE IN THE WIND.

HAAH! HAAH! HAAH!

YEP!

SWF

WAS IT?

KAMIYA-SAN...

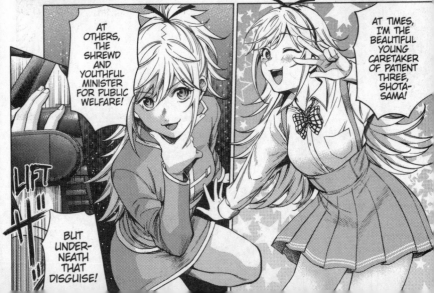

AT OTHERS, THE SHREWD AND YOUTHFUL MINISTER FOR PUBLIC WELFARE!

AT TIMES, I'M THE BEAUTIFUL YOUNG CARETAKER OF PATIENT THREE, SHOTA-SAMA!

LIFT

BUT UNDERNEATH THAT DISGUISE!

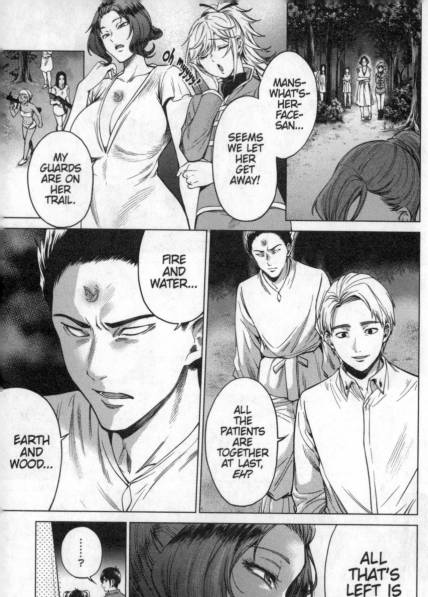

Oh myyyy!

MANS-WHAT'S-HER-FACE-SAN...

SEEMS WE LET HER GET AWAY!

MY GUARDS ARE ON HER TRAIL.

FIRE AND WATER...

EARTH AND WOOD...

ALL THE PATIENTS ARE TOGETHER AT LAST, EH?

......?

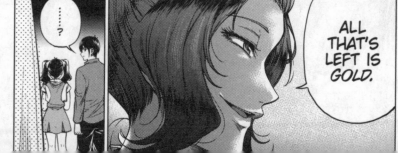

ALL THAT'S LEFT IS GOLD.

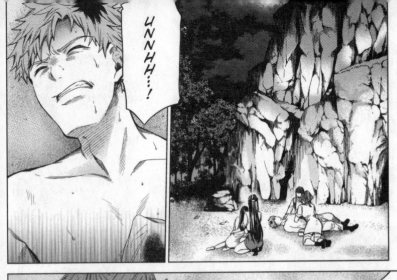

UNNHH...!

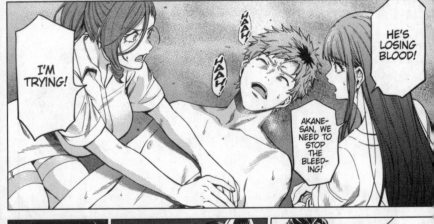

HE'S LOSING BLOOD!

I'M TRYING!

HAAH!

HAAH!

AKANE-SAN, WE NEED TO STOP THE BLEEDING!

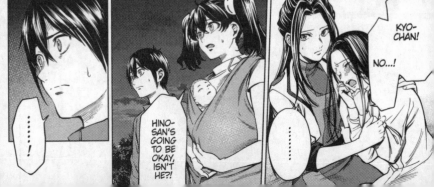

.....!

HINO-SAN'S GOING TO BE OKAY, ISN'T HE?!

KYO-CHAN!

NO...!

.....!

HAAAH...
HAAAH...
Rustle...
Rustle...
DAMN!
THUMP
HAAH...
HAAAH...!
HAAAH...
HAAAH...
THOSE DAMN JAPS!

# Ch. 85 Brave New World

world's end harem

IT'S IZANAMI!

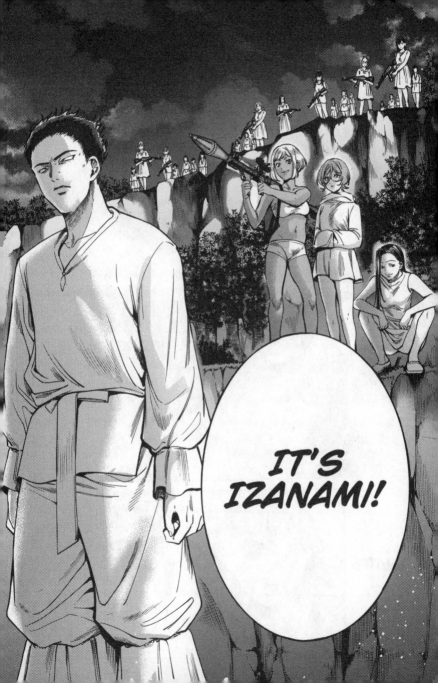

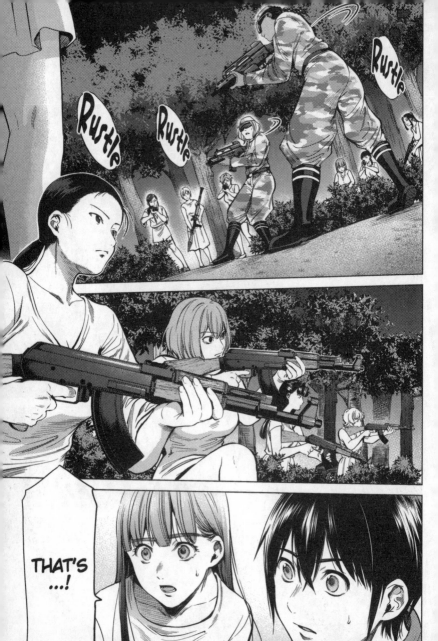

Rustle

Rustle

Rustle

THAT'S
...!

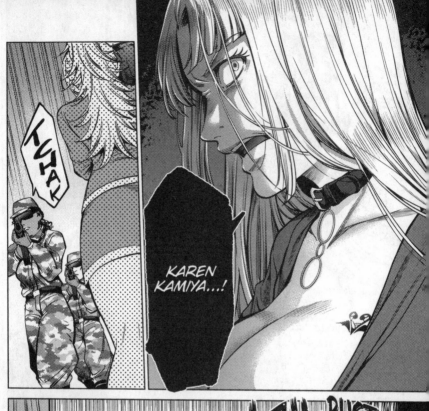

TCHAK

KAREN KAMIYA....!

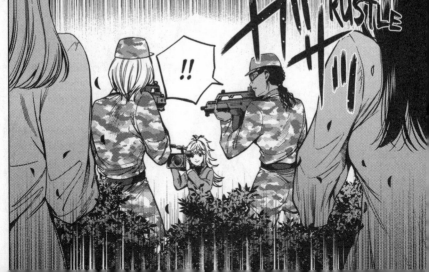

!!

RUSTLE

AAAAND CUT!
NICE WORK, EVERY-BODY!
MANS-WHAT'S-YOUR-NAME-SAN!
THAT EXPRES-SION WAS PRIIICE-LESS!
I THINK WE'VE GOT EVERY-THING WE NEED. ★

BANG
??!!
WHAT THE FU--!

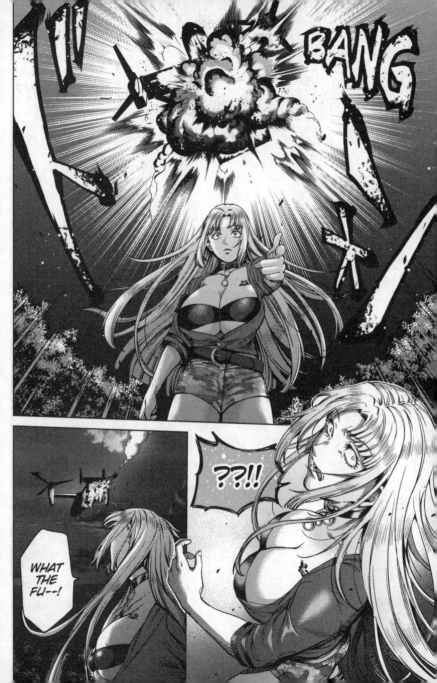

TCHAKA-CHAKA-CHAKA
!!
CHAKA
CHAKA-CHAKA
ウィィン…
Whirr…
……!
FIRE.

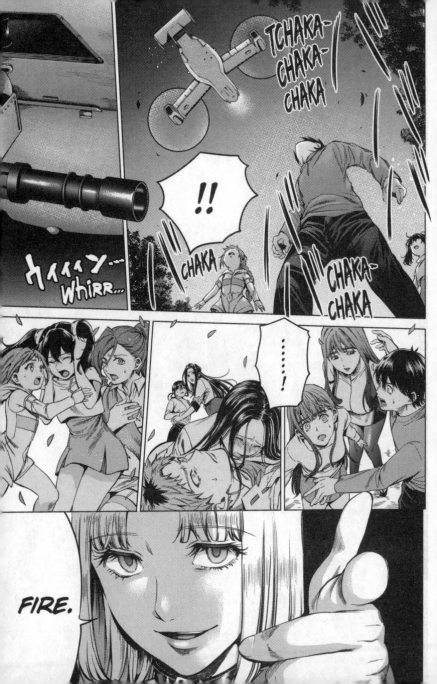

KYO-CHAN!
KYO-CHAN!!
YUKARI... I'M F-FINE!
HAAAH
HAAAH
LISTEN, THE BABY...!
UNLESS WE TREAT HIM SOON...
HINO-SAN'S GOING TO DIE!
WELL.
NOW THAT I'VE TOLD YOU ALL MY SECRETS.
REGRET-TABLY, IT'S TIME...
TO ERASE MIZU-HARA-SAN FROM HISTORY!
RAISE

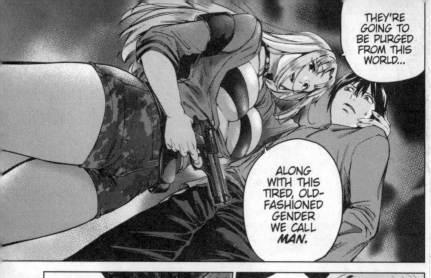

THEY'RE GOING TO BE PURGED FROM THIS WORLD...

ALONG WITH THIS TIRED, OLD-FASHIONED GENDER WE CALL *MAN*.

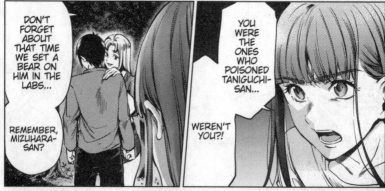

DON'T FORGET ABOUT THAT TIME WE SET A BEAR ON HIM IN THE LABS...

REMEMBER, MIZUHARA-SAN?

YOU WERE THE ONES WHO POISONED TANIGUCHI-SAN...

WEREN'T YOU?!

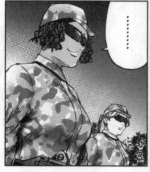

· · · · · · ·

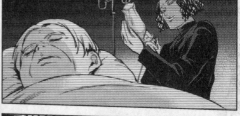

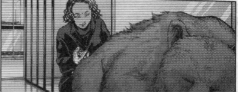

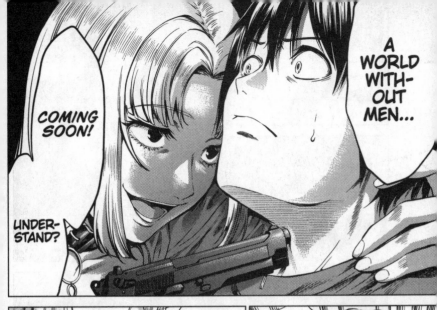

A WORLD WITH- OUT MEN...

COMING SOON!

UNDER- STAND?

WE HUMANS CREATED SCIENCE TO FIGHT AGAINST THE UNREASONABLE MOTHER NATURE...

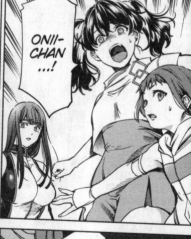

ONII- CHAN ....!

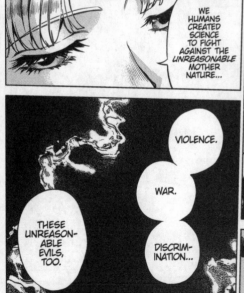

VIOLENCE.

WAR.

DISCRIM- INATION...

THESE UNREASON- ABLE EVILS, TOO.

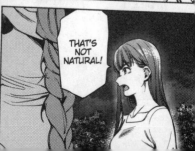

THAT'S NOT NATURAL!

I...
I...
I WANTED IT!
I KNEW IT.
!!
ザッ Tmp
ザッ Tmp
WE'VE NO USE FOR YOU ANY-MORE.
WE'RE GETTING OUR LABS READY TO REPRODUCE WITHOUT MALES, OVER IN THE STATES.

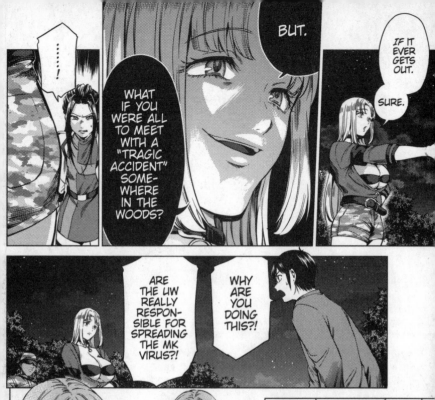

......!

BUT.

WHAT IF YOU WERE ALL TO MEET WITH A "TRAGIC ACCIDENT" SOMEWHERE IN THE WOODS?

IF IT EVER GETS OUT.

SURE.

ARE THE UW REALLY RESPONSIBLE FOR SPREADING THE MK VIRUS?!

WHY ARE YOU DOING THIS?!

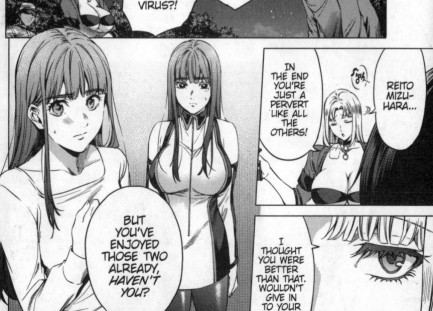

IN THE END YOU'RE JUST A PERVERT LIKE ALL THE OTHERS!

*sigh...*

REITO MIZU-HARA...

BUT YOU'VE ENJOYED THOSE TWO ALREADY, HAVEN'T YOU?

I THOUGHT YOU WERE BETTER THAN THAT. WOULDN'T GIVE IN TO YOUR LIBIDO.

ONE MORE STEP...
AND YOU'LL ALL BE FULL OF HOLES.
GH...!
IF IT EVER GETS OUT THAT YOU'VE HURT THE PATIENTS...
THE WORLD WILL NEVER FORGIVE YOU!

YOU TOOK THE SHORT-CUT...
JUST AS WE EXPECTED.
CHLOE ...
MANS-FIELD!
WE HAVE TO STOP THE BLEEDING!
——!!
DON'T ...
MOVE...!

KYO-CHAN ...?!
KYO-CHAAN!
CRASH
H...
HINO-SAN!!
OOPS.
I MISSED ONE.

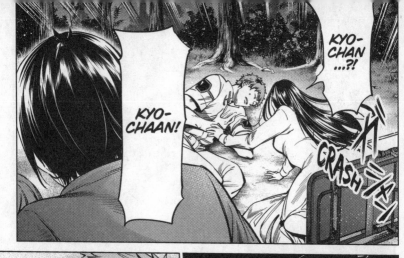

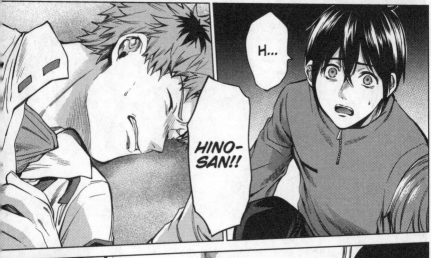

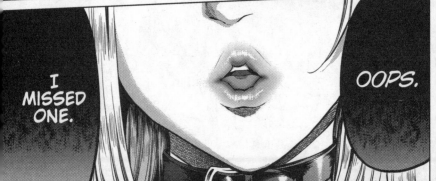

UH...
NH...
THMP
SOAK...

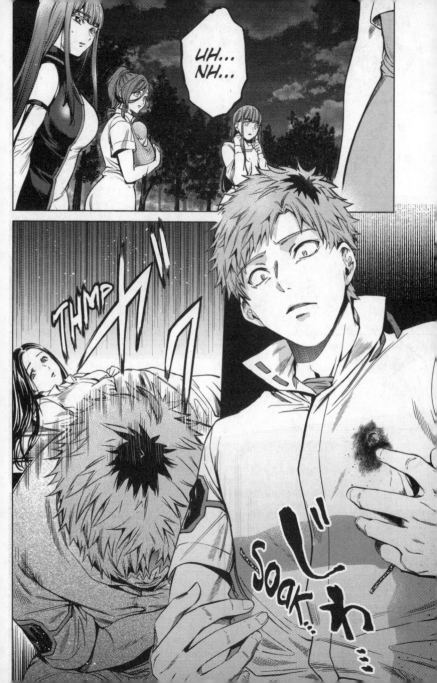

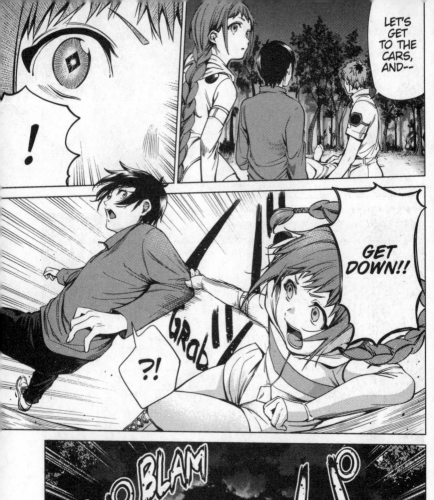

LET'S GET TO THE CARS, AND--

!

GET DOWN!!

Grab

?!

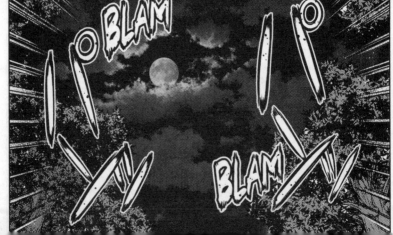

I KNEW THEY'D FIND US EVENTU-ALLY, BUT...
NOT THIS QUICKLY!
I CAN SEE THE EXIT!
ALL RIGHT!
I THINK WE LOST 'EM NOW!

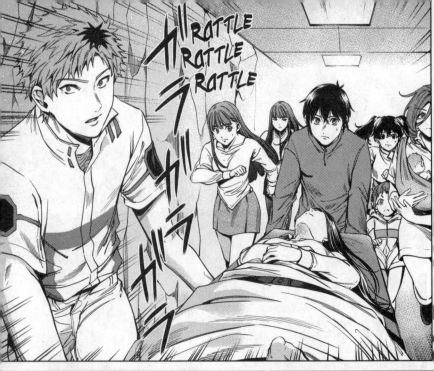

RATTLE
RATTLE
RATTLE

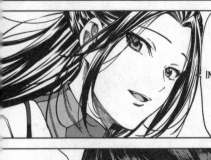

WE'RE LUCKY YOU INFILTRATED THAT REFUGEE DISTRICT!

FORTUNATELY I NOTICED THEIR HELICOPTER COMING IN TO ATTACK.

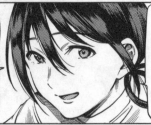

I WANTED TO BE WITH ONEE-SAMA, BUT...

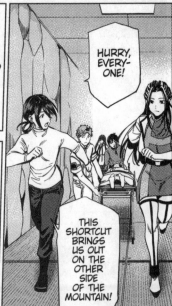

HURRY, EVERYONE!

THIS SHORTCUT BRINGS US OUT ON THE OTHER SIDE OF THE MOUNTAIN!

WHAM!!
!!!
Empty...
がらん...
Tch!
No one's here.

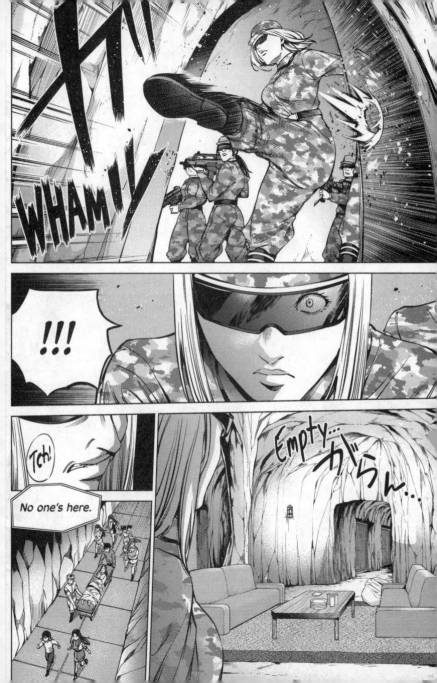

WHAT'S THAT NOISE?
THAT ALERT MEANS SOME-BODY'S HERE.

......

HALT

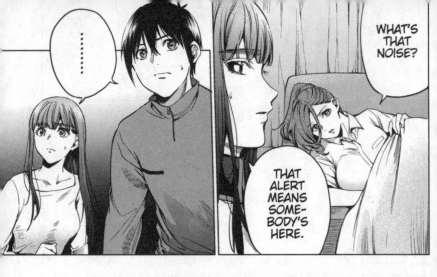

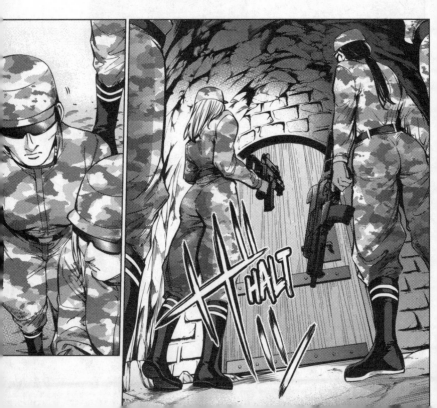

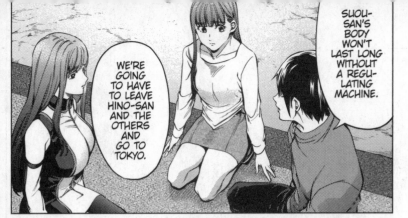

WE'RE GOING TO HAVE TO LEAVE HINO-SAN AND THE OTHERS AND GO TO TOKYO.

SHOU-SAN'S BODY WON'T LAST LONG WITHOUT A REGU-LATING MACHINE.

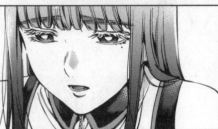

I CAN'T HAVE EVERYONE EXPOSED TO DANGER LIKE THAT FOR MY SAKE.

BUT I...

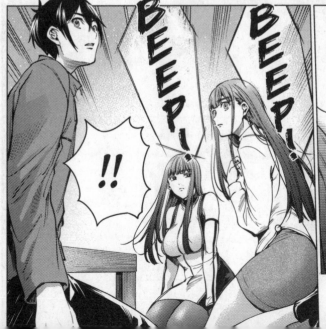

BEEP!

BEEP!

!!

ACTUALLY, I HAVE AN IDEA.

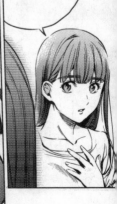

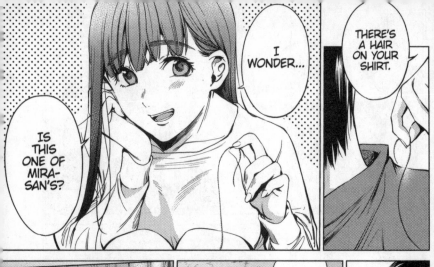

THERE'S A HAIR ON YOUR SHIRT.

I WONDER...

IS THIS ONE OF MIRA-SAN'S?

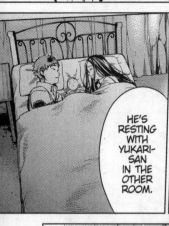

HE'S RESTING WITH YUKARI-SAN IN THE OTHER ROOM.

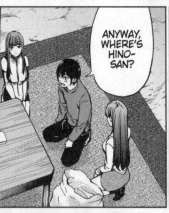

ANYWAY, WHERE'S HINO-SAN?

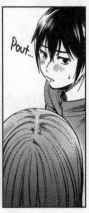

Pout...

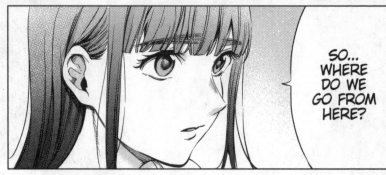

SO... WHERE DO WE GO FROM HERE?

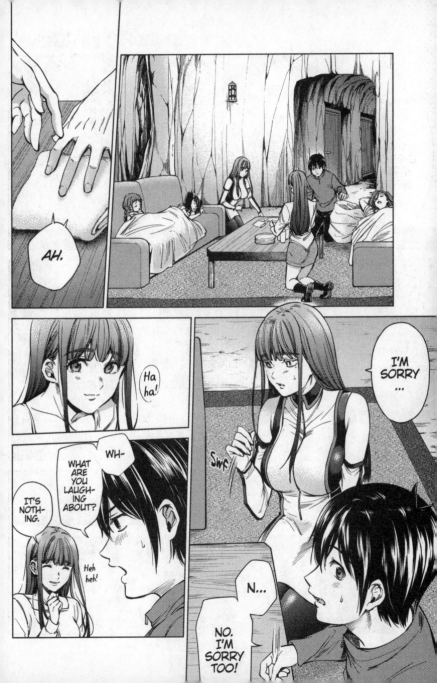

AH.

Ha ha!

WH- WHAT ARE YOU LAUGH- ING ABOUT?

IT'S NOTH- ING.

Heh heh!

I'M SORRY ...

SWF

N...

NO. I'M SORRY TOO!

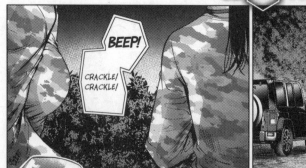

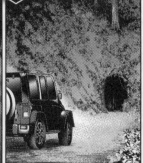

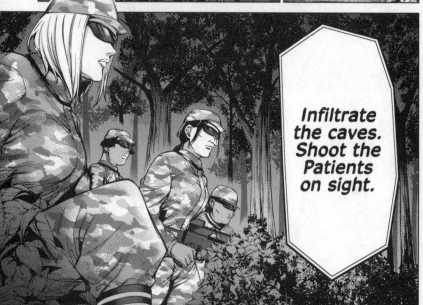

*Infiltrate the caves. Shoot the Patients on sight.*

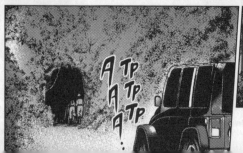

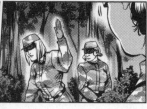

world's end harem

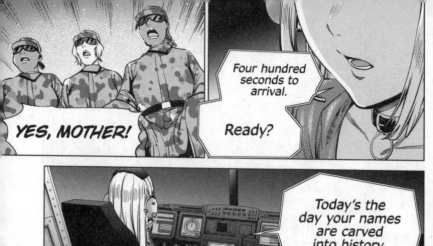

Four hundred seconds to arrival.

YES, MOTHER!

Ready?

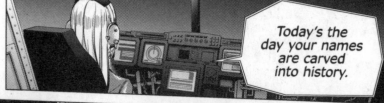

Today's the day your names are carved into history.

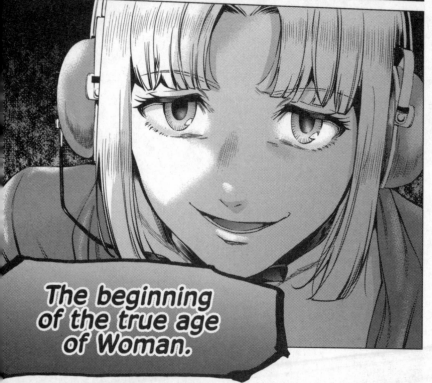

The beginning of the true age of Woman.

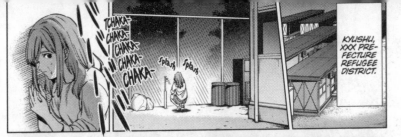

TCHAKA-
CHAKA-
CHAKA-
CHAKA-
CHAKA-

Splash Splash

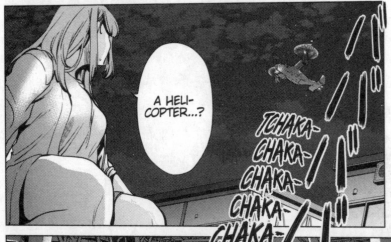

A HELI-COPTER...?

TCHAKA-
CHAKA-
CHAKA-
CHAKA-
CHAKA-

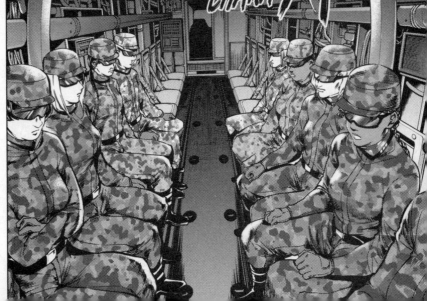

NH... REITO-SAMA...
LICK
YOU TOO, MIRA-SAN?
Ahn!
REITO... LET'S COME TOGETHER ...!
Haah!
Haah!
THRUST
THRUST
THRUST
Ahh!
ELISA...!
HNNAH...!
Ahh!
TWITCH
Squeeze
TWITCH

YOU'RE NOT DONE YET, ARE YOU?
Perk up ♥
YOU'RE REALLY... AGGRES-SIVE TONIGHT, ELISA...
I WOULDN'T ...
DO THIS FOR JUST ANYONE, OKAY?
Shf

NH...
Kiss
MIRA-SAN...
I... I'M GONNA ...!
Haah!
Haah!
Haah!
Ah!
REITO-SAMA...!
Spasm
Twitch
HAAH!
HAAH!
WHAT, TIRED AL-READY?

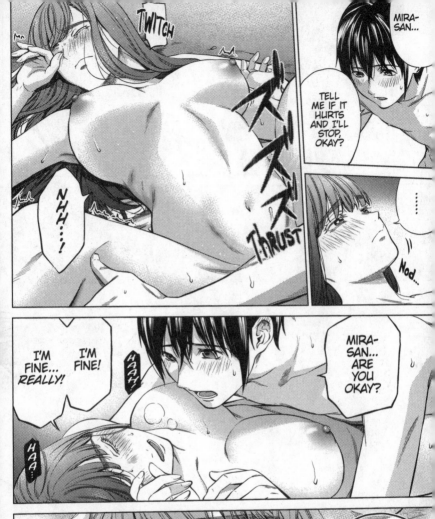

TWITCH

MIRA-SAN...

TELL ME IF IT HURTS AND I'LL STOP, OKAY?

NHH...!

THRUST

......

Nod...

I'M FINE... REALLY!

I'M FINE!

HAAH!

HAA...!

MIRA-SAN... ARE YOU OKAY?

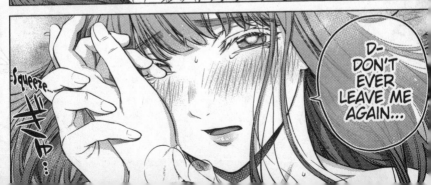

Squeeze...

D-DON'T EVER LEAVE ME AGAIN...

ARE YOU SURE?
YOU WANT ME TO GO FIRST?
ba-dmp
OF COURSE.
ba-dmp
REITO...
BE GENTLE, WON'T YOU?

NH...
NHH...!
TWITCH
Kiss
Lick
NHAAA...!
AHH!
Kiss
Suck
AHN!♥
HAAAH!
REITO... THAT FEELS SO GOOD!
REITO-SAMA!
MIRA-SAN!
Lick
Kiss...

Haah!
Haah!
LYING HERE WITH TWO BEAUTIFUL WOMEN AT THE END OF THE WORLD...
YOU'VE GOT YOUR VERY OWN HAREM, REITO.
DON'T MAKE FUN OF ME.
REITO...
Kiss...
I LOVE YOU.

b-dmp
b-dmp
b-dmp
REITO.
ba-dmp
ba-dmp
R...
REITO-SAMA.
PLEASE, GIVE ME YOUR LOVE...
......!
Kiss...
......
Kiss Kiss

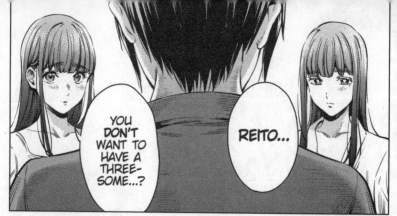

YOU DON'T WANT TO HAVE A THREE-SOME...?

REITO...

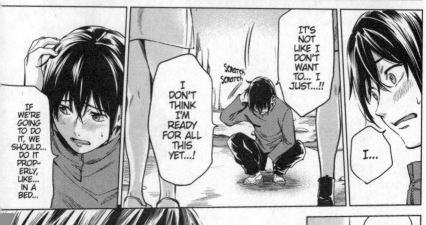

IF WE'RE GOING TO DO IT, WE SHOULD... DO IT PROPERLY, LIKE... IN A BED...

I DON'T THINK I'M READY FOR ALL THIS YET...!

Scratch Scratch

IT'S NOT LIKE I DON'T WANT TO... I JUST...!!

I...

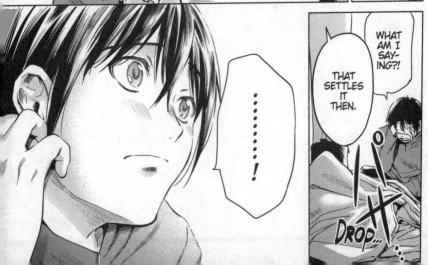

..........!

WHAT AM I SAY-ING?!

THAT SETTLES IT THEN.

DROP...

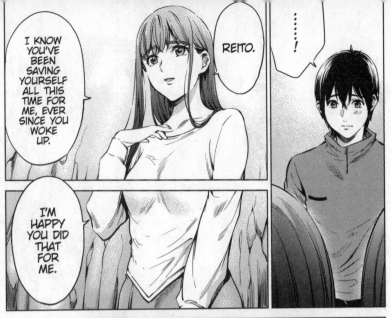

I KNOW YOU'VE BEEN SAVING YOURSELF ALL THIS TIME FOR ME, EVER SINCE YOU WOKE UP.

REITO.

...!

I'M HAPPY YOU DID THAT FOR ME.

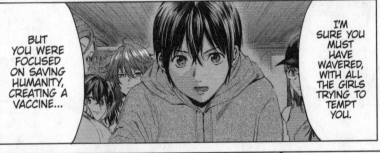

BUT YOU WERE FOCUSED ON SAVING HUMANITY, CREATING A VACCINE...

I'M SURE YOU MUST HAVE WAVERED, WITH ALL THE GIRLS TRYING TO TEMPT YOU.

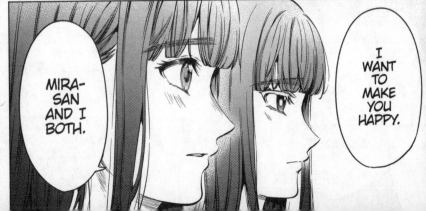

MIRA-SAN AND I BOTH.

I WANT TO MAKE YOU HAPPY.

BACK THEN...
IT TOOK ALL MY COURAGE JUST TO WALK THROUGH THE DOOR.
St- stop...!!
I WAS REALLY UPSET BY IT, YOU KNOW?
I... I'M SORRY...
I'M ONLY HALF JOKING.
BUT TACHIBANA-SAN...
ELISA-SAN. I'M SERIOUS ABOUT WANTING HER TO BE WITH YOU, TOO.
MIZUHARA-SAMA...
IF... YOU CAN FIND IT IN YOURSELF TO DO SO.
WILL YOU TRY TO THINK OF ELISA-SAN AND I...
AS ONE WOMAN IN TWO BODIES?

I THOUGHT YOU WANTED ME AND SUOU-SAN TO DO IT?!
AH, NO!
I HAVEN'T AGREED, IT'S JUST...
I...
I THOUGHT YOU JUST WANTED IT TO BE ME AND HER!
THAT WAS MY INTEN-TION AT FIRST!
I SUGGESTED IT.
!
I...
IT'S MY FIRST TIME HAVING INTER-COURSE WITH A MALE, AND...
TO BE HONEST, I'M NERVOUS.
DO YOU REMEMBER WHEN WE FIRST MET? I CAME INTO YOUR ROOM AT NIGHT...
?!
JOLT
EH?!
AH, OF COURSE. I REMEMBER.

I MEAN... UNLESS WE DO THIS NOW, YOU'RE NEVER GOING TO DO IT WITH ANYBODY ELSE AGAIN, ARE YOU?
WELL.
YEAH... I WASN'T PLANNING ON IT.
AND WELL... I HAVE ANOTHER PROPOSAL, IF YOU'LL LISTEN.
WHAT IS IT?
I THOUGHT...
MAYBE WE COULD DO IT TOGETHER.
ALL THREE OF US.
ALL THREE OF US??!!

JUST AS I TOLD YOU...
MIRA-SAN AND I HAVE THE SAME GENETIC MAKEUP.
......
SO I...
FEEL THAT HER AND I ARE CONNECTED. OUR MINDS ARE ONE.
TH...
THAT DOESN'T MAKE ANY SENSE!
ELISA... SHE'S INCREDIBLY STUB-BORN WHEN SHE WANTS TO BE!

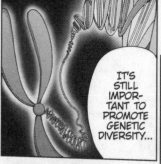

IT'S STILL IMPORTANT TO PROMOTE GENETIC DIVERSITY...

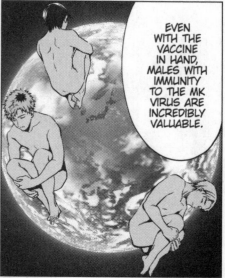

EVEN WITH THE VACCINE IN HAND, MALES WITH IMMUNITY TO THE MK VIRUS ARE INCREDIBLY VALUABLE.

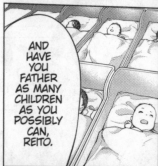

AND HAVE YOU FATHER AS MANY CHILDREN AS YOU POSSIBLY CAN, REITO.

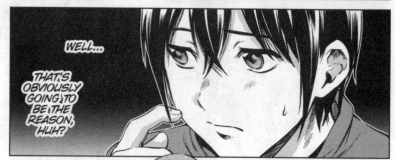

WELL...

THAT'S OBVIOUSLY GOING TO BE THE REASON, HUH?

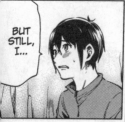

BUT STILL, I...

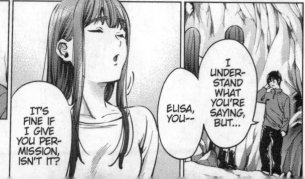

IT'S FINE IF I GIVE YOU PER-MISSION, ISN'T IT?

ELISA, YOU--

I UNDER-STAND WHAT YOU'RE SAYING, BUT...

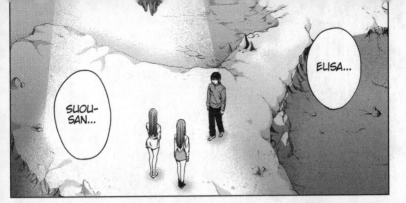

ELISA...

SUOU-SAN...

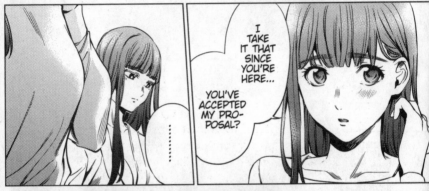

I TAKE IT THAT SINCE YOU'RE HERE...

YOU'VE ACCEPTED MY PROPOSAL?

.........

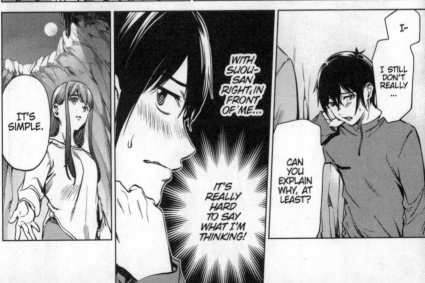

IT'S SIMPLE.

WITH SUOU-SAN RIGHT IN FRONT OF ME...

IT'S REALLY HARD TO SAY WHAT I'M THINKING!

I-

I STILL DON'T REALLY...

CAN YOU EXPLAIN WHY, AT LEAST?

THIS IS...!
!
Tmp...
Tmp...
Tmp...

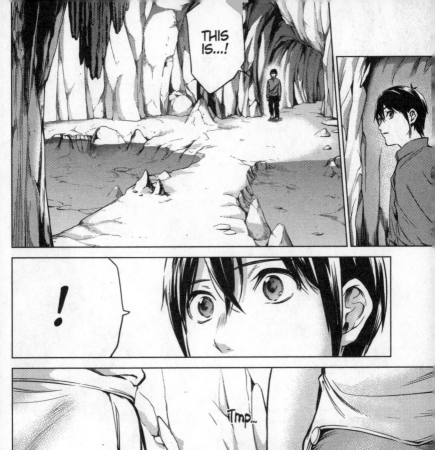

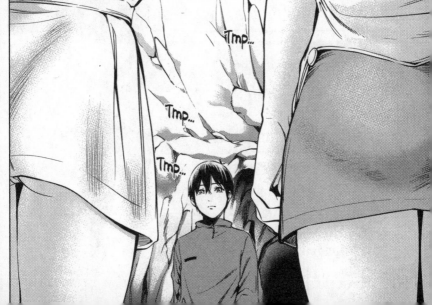

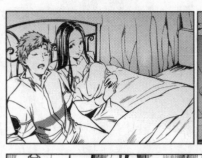

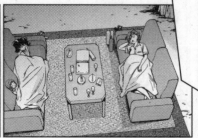

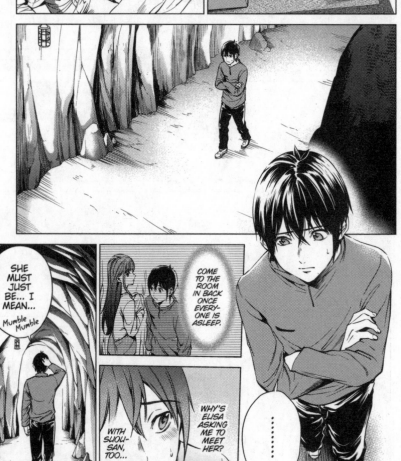

COME TO THE ROOM IN BACK ONCE EVERY-ONE IS ASLEEP.

SHE MUST JUST BE... I MEAN...

Mumble Mumble

WHY'S ELISA ASKING ME TO MEET HER?

WITH SHOU-SAN, TOO...

· · · · · · · ·

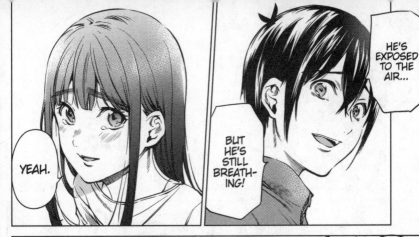

YEAH.

HE'S EXPOSED TO THE AIR...

BUT HE'S STILL BREATHING!

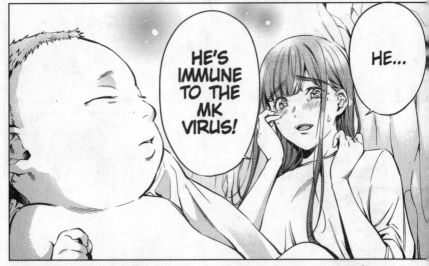

HE'S IMMUNE TO THE MK VIRUS!

HE...

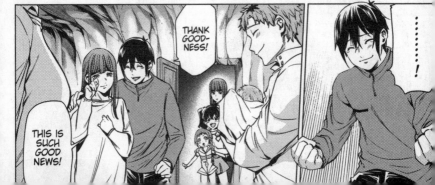

THANK GOODNESS!

THIS IS SUCH GOOD NEWS!

.........!

HE LOOKS JUST LIKE HIS DAD!
Waaa-aahhh!
!!

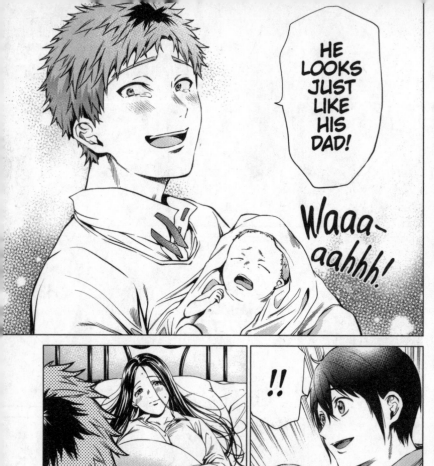

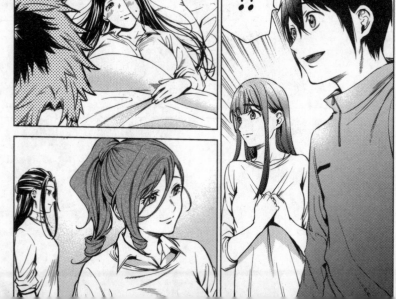

H...
HINO-SAN?
SOB...
......!
MIZU-HARA-KUN...
Mmh
HE...

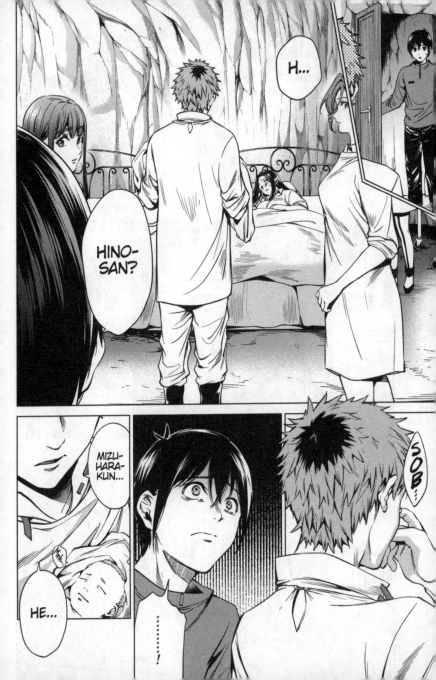

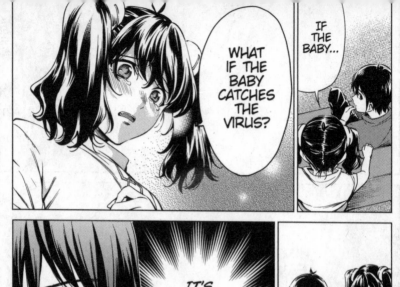

WHAT IF THE BABY CATCHES THE VIRUS?

IF THE BABY...

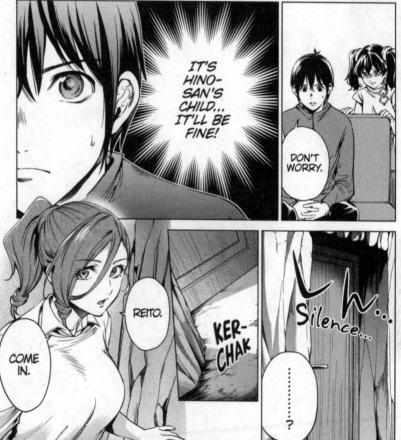

IT'S HINO-SAN'S CHILD... IT'LL BE FINE!

DON'T WORRY.

REITO.

COME IN.

KER-CHAK

Silence...

......?

I CAN SEE THE HEAD!
JUST A LITTLE MORE ...!
JUST ONE MORE PUSH, YUKARI!
YUKARI!
ONE MORE!
WAAAAAHH!
I HOPE SHE'S OKAY...
ALL WE CAN DO IS WAIT.
......

UHHNNN!!
WAAAH!
WAAAAAAAHHHH!!
Ch. 83 Two
HAAAH!
HAAH!
PUSH!
AAHHHH!!
YUKARI... YOU CAN DO THIS!
YOU CAN DO IT!
HFF!
HFF!
NHHH!
NNNHHH!

I WANT YOU...
TO MATE WITH REITO.

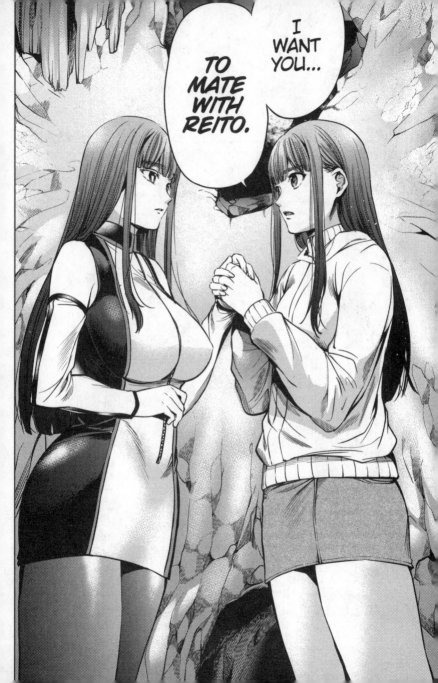

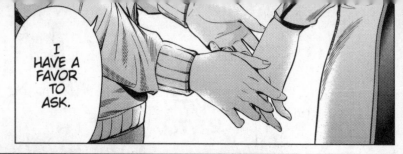

I HAVE A FAVOR TO ASK.

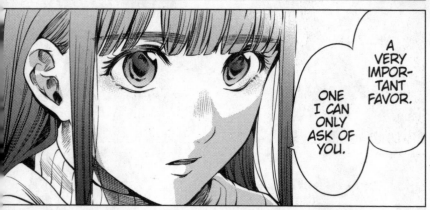

A VERY IMPORTANT FAVOR.

ONE I CAN ONLY ASK OF YOU.

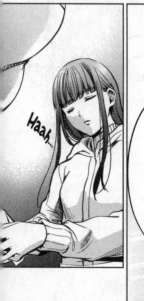

Haah...

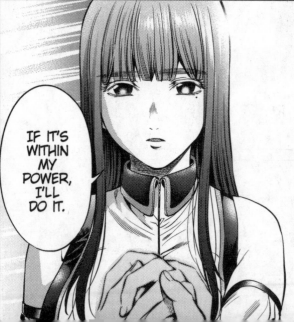

IF IT'S WITHIN MY POWER, I'LL DO IT.

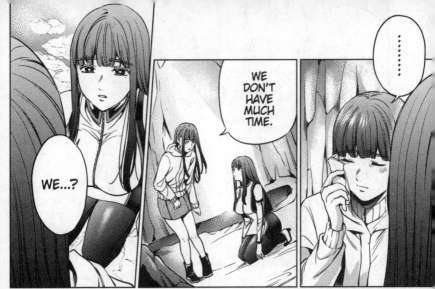

WE...?

WE DON'T HAVE MUCH TIME.

.......

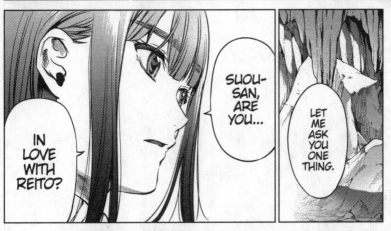

IN LOVE WITH REITO?

SUOU-SAN, ARE YOU...

LET ME ASK YOU ONE THING.

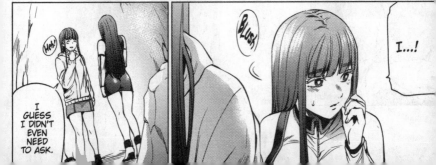

Heh!

I GUESS I DIDN'T EVEN NEED TO ASK.

BLUSH

I....!

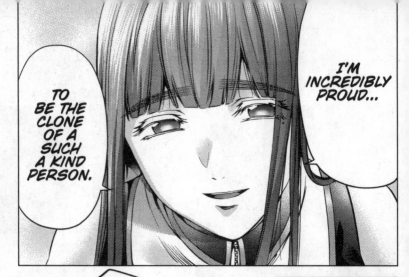

I'M INCREDIBLY PROUD...

TO BE THE CLONE OF A SUCH A KIND PERSON.

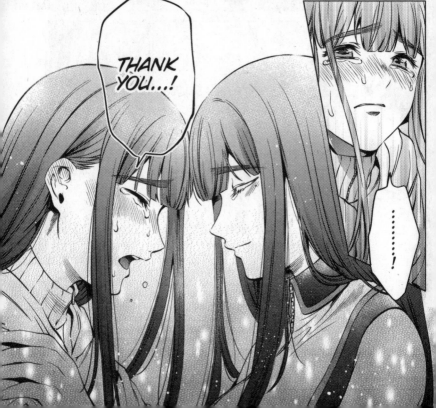

THANK YOU...!

.........!

I...
I'D ALWAYS WANTED TO MEET YOU SOME-DAY.
I WAS A LITTLE SCARED THAT YOU'D BE ANGRY WITH ME OVER THE MIZUHARA-SAMA SITUATION...
I'M SO GLAD TO FIND YOU'RE SUCH A GOOD PERSON.
YOU'D EVEN CRY FOR ME.
I AM HERE BECAUSE I CHOSE TO BE.
AND...

YOU...
IT'S ALL MY FAULT!
I-I DON'T EVEN KNOW WHAT TO SAY...
I'M SO SORRY!
I...
I HAVE NO RIGHT TO CRY IN FRONT OF YOU.
GOOD.

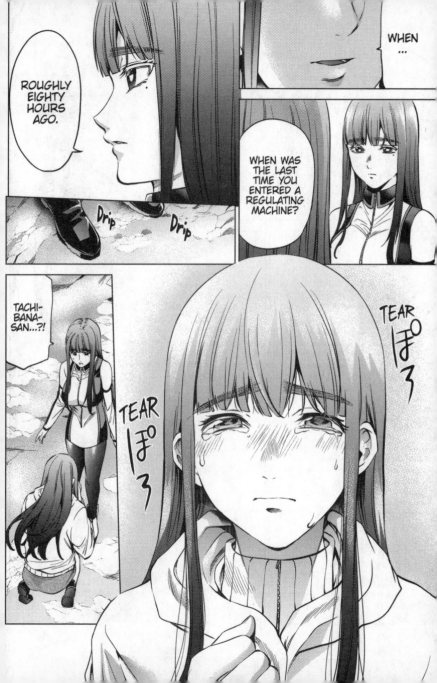

WHEN
...

ROUGHLY EIGHTY HOURS AGO.

WHEN WAS THE LAST TIME YOU ENTERED A REGULATING MACHINE?

Drip

Drip

TACHI-BANA-SAN...?!

TEAR
ぽ
ろ

TEAR
ぽ
ろ

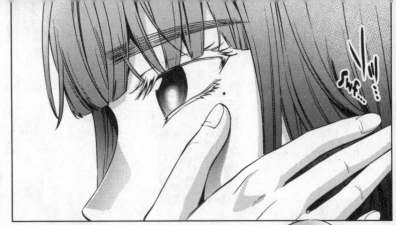

SWf...

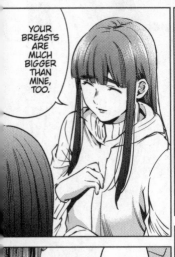

YOUR BREASTS ARE MUCH BIGGER THAN MINE, TOO.

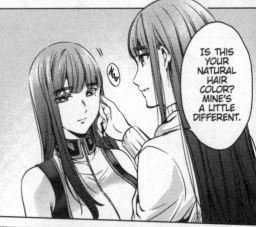

*Nod*

IS THIS YOUR NATURAL HAIR COLOR? MINE'S A LITTLE DIFFERENT.

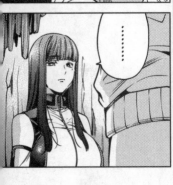

. . . . . . . .

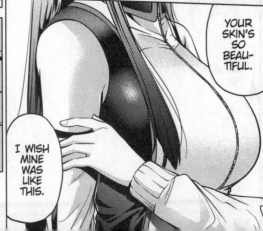

YOUR SKIN'S SO BEAUTIFUL.

I WISH MINE WAS LIKE THIS.

CAN I...
TOUCH YOU?
GO AHEAD.

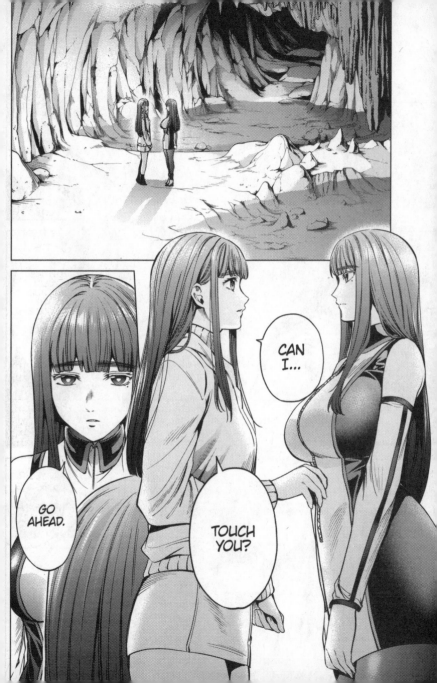

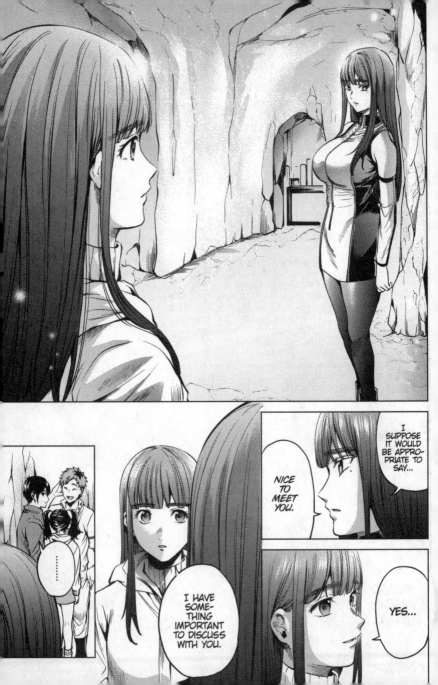

I SUPPOSE IT WOULD BE APPROPRIATE TO SAY...

NICE TO MEET YOU.

.........

I HAVE SOMETHING IMPORTANT TO DISCUSS WITH YOU.

YES...

YO!
MR. SAVIOR OF HUMANITY IN THE HOUSE!
HINO-SAN!
MIZU-HARA-KUN!
HUG
GOOD TO SEE YOU, MAN!
YOU... REALLY CAME ALL THIS WAY, *HUH*?
YOU'RE CUTE AS EVER TOO, MAHIRU-CHAN!
MIRA, IT'S BEEN TOO LONG.
LONG TIME NO SEE!
AKANE-SAN, SUI-SAN.
I'M HAPPY TO SEE YOU BOTH IN GOOD HEALTH.
SUOU MIRA-SAN.

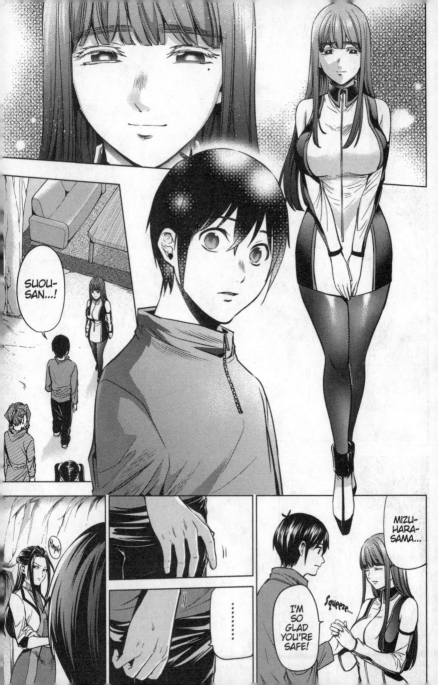

SUOU-SAN...!

MIZU-HARA-SAMA...

I'M SO GLAD YOU'RE SAFE!

Squeeze...

THIS IS IT.
!
WHOA...
THERE'S A WHOLE HOME DOWN HERE!
WE'VE BEEN WAITING.

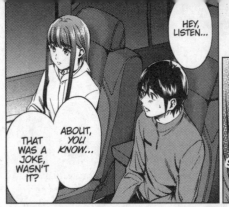

HEY, LISTEN...

THAT WAS A JOKE, WASN'T IT?

ABOUT, YOU KNOW...

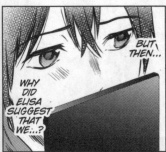

BUT THEN...

WHY DID ELISA SUGGEST THAT WE...?

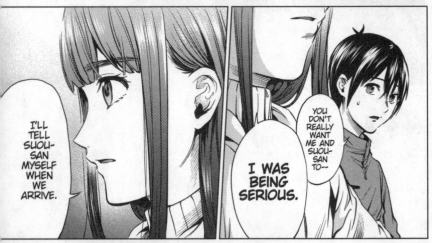

I'LL TELL SUOU-SAN MYSELF WHEN WE ARRIVE.

I WAS BEING SERIOUS.

YOU DON'T REALLY WANT ME AND SUOU-SAN TO--

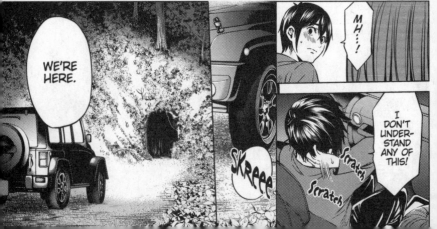

WE'RE HERE.

MH...!

I DON'T UNDERSTAND ANY OF THIS!

SKREEE

Scratch

Scratch

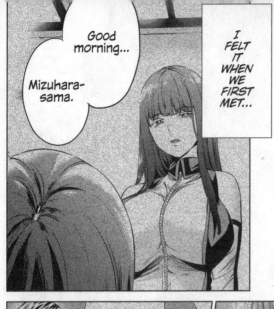

Good morning...

Mizuhara-sama.

I FELT IT WHEN WE FIRST MET...

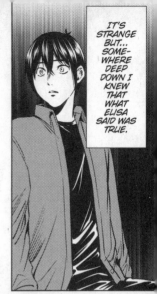

IT'S STRANGE BUT... SOMEWHERE DEEP DOWN I KNEW THAT WHAT ELISA SAID WAS TRUE.

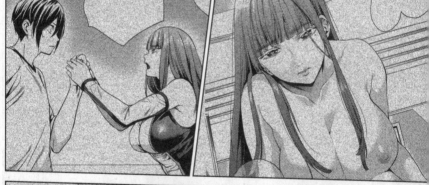

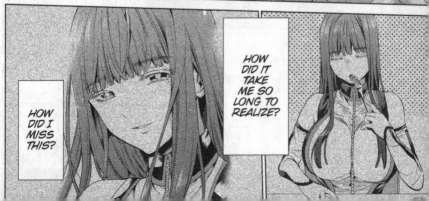

HOW DID I MISS THIS?

HOW DID IT TAKE ME SO LONG TO REALIZE?

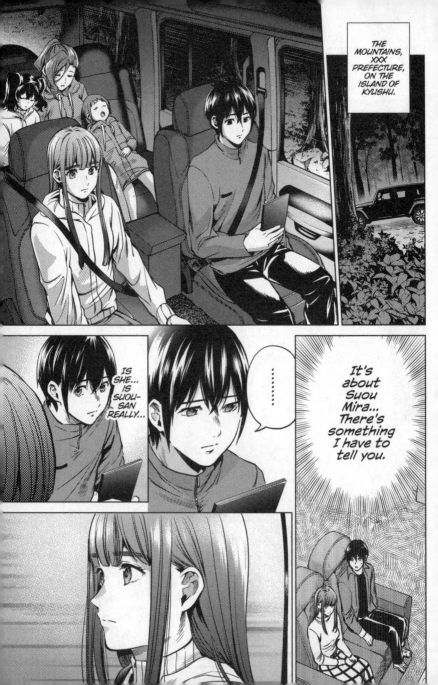

THE MOUNTAINS, XXX PREFECTURE, ON THE ISLAND OF KYUSHU.

IS SHE... IS SUOU-SAN REALLY...

· · · · ·

It's about Suou Mira... There's something I have to tell you.

PLEASE...
PROTECT US!
.......!
SQUEEZE...
WE CAN'T BEAT THEM ON OUR OWN.
THEY LEAVE US NO OTHER CHOICE.
GRIN

HMM...
FIRST MIZUHARA-SAN, NOW HINO-SAN.
THOSE FOREIGNERS...
MIGHT RESORT TO SERIOUS ACTION, YOU KNOW.
THEIR GOAL IS TO ELIMINATE ALL MEN FROM THIS WORLD.
NOW THAT THEY'RE UNABLE TO CONTROL HINO-SAN, THEY MAY JUST...
......
SHOTA-SAMA...
WHAT SHOULD WE DO?
......
DOI-KUN...

TO DECEIVE YOUR ENEMY, FIRST YOU'VE GOTTA DECEIVE YOUR FRIENDS! ★
I SEE...
THANKS FOR KEEPING SENSEI SAFE, EVEN IF IT WAS JUST YOUR WAY OF TRYING TO CONTROL ME.
EH?!
GOSH, THAT'S SUCH A MEANY WAY OF PUTTING IT!
ANY-WAY.
RIGHT NOW, MANS-WHAT'S-HER-NAME-SAN AND HER FRIENDS ARE HEADING THIS WAY.
WHAT DOES SHE WANT IN JAPAN?
PATIENT ONE HAS ESCAPED, ALONG WITH A WOMAN PREGNANT WITH HIS BABY BOY.
!
ALL OF PATIENT TWO'S FORMER CARETAKERS HAVE DISAPPEARED, TOO. THE JAPAN BRANCH IS PANICKING.

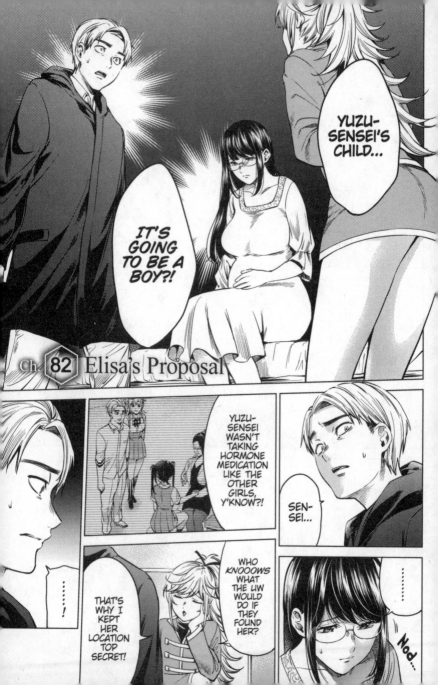

YUZU-SENSEI'S CHILD...

IT'S GOING TO BE A BOY?!

Ch. 82 Elisa's Proposal

YUZU-SENSEI WASN'T TAKING HORMONE MEDICATION LIKE THE OTHER GIRLS, Y'KNOW?!

SEN-SEI...

WHO KNOOOWS WHAT THE UW WOULD DO IF THEY FOUND HER?

......!

THAT'S WHY I KEPT HER LOCATION TOP SECRET!

Nod...

world's end harem

AH!
WHAT IS IT?
I HAVE ANOTHER ANNOUNCEMENT TO MAKE!
THE LITTLE BABY IN SENSEI'S TUMMY...
IT'S A BOY! ★

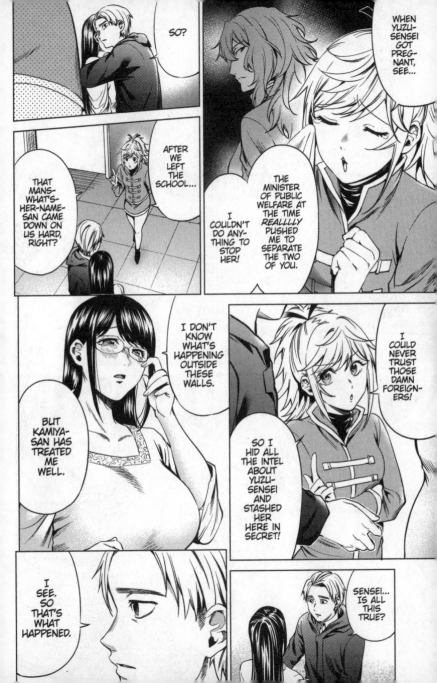

SO?

WHEN YUZU-SENSEI GOT PREGNANT, SEE...

AFTER WE LEFT THE SCHOOL...

THE MINISTER OF PUBLIC WELFARE AT THE TIME *REALLLY* PUSHED ME TO SEPARATE THE TWO OF YOU.

THAT MAN'S—WHAT'S-HER-NAME-SAN CAME DOWN ON US HARD, RIGHT?

I COULDN'T DO ANYTHING TO STOP HER!

I DON'T KNOW WHAT'S HAPPENING OUTSIDE THESE WALLS.

I COULD NEVER TRUST THOSE DAMN FOREIGNERS!

BUT KAMIYA-SAN HAS TREATED ME WELL.

SO I HID ALL THE INTEL ABOUT YUZU-SENSEI AND STASHED HER HERE IN SECRET!

I SEE. SO THAT'S WHAT HAPPENED.

SENSEI... IS ALL THIS TRUE?

SENSEI... WHY...
Tmp
Tmp
!
YOUR BELLY...!
DOI-KUN!
......!
I... I...!
Grasp...
I'M SO GLAD YOU'RE OKAY.
IT'S SO GOOD TO SEE YOU!

DOI-KUN...?!
SENSEI!

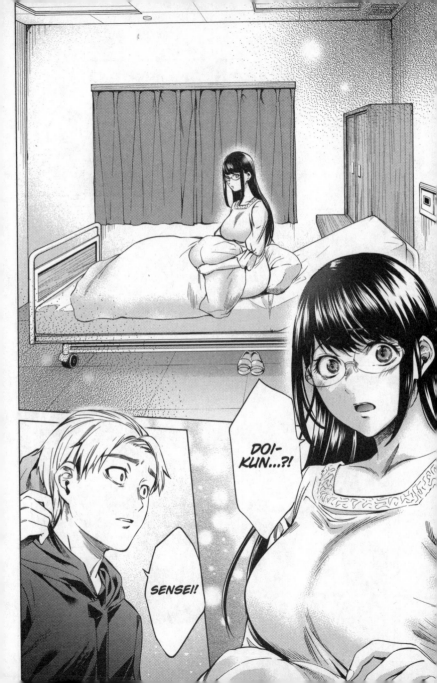

IT'S JUST A REGULAR TREATMENT FACILITY FOR FEMALE REFUGEES.

WHY WOULD SHE BRING ME HERE?

KEEP YOUR VOICE DOWN, OKAY?

Shh...

KER-chak...

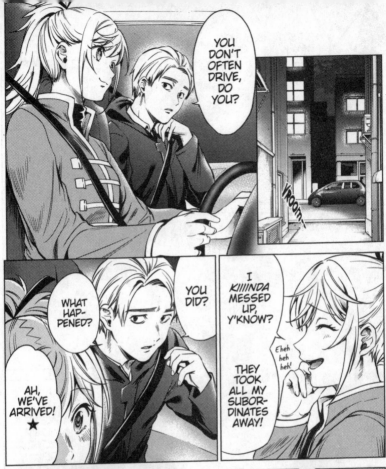

YOU DON'T OFTEN DRIVE, DO YOU?

VROOM...

WHAT HAP-PENED?

YOU DID?

I KIIIINDA MESSED UP, Y'KNOW?

Eheh heh heh!

AH, WE'VE ARRIVED! ★

THEY TOOK ALL MY SUBOR-DINATES AWAY!

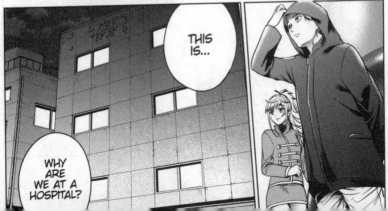

THIS IS...

WHY ARE WE AT A HOSPITAL?

HEY... YOU ALL... NH!
Ah!♥
IT'S... MN--! MY TURN NOW...!
Ahn!
YOU GUYS ARE THE BEST...!

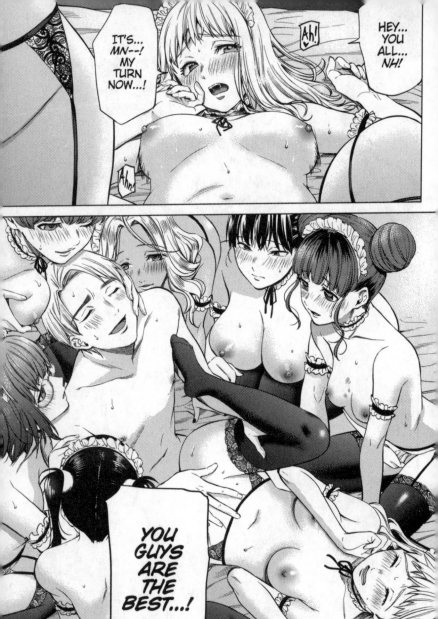

HERE GOES...
MASTER-SAMA...!
AHHH...!
THRUST
HURRY UP AND DO ME...
HAAH!
HAAH...
HAAH!
I'M SECOND!
HAAH!
Ahh!
MASTER-SAMA...
HAAH!
Ahn!

WE ALL DECIDED ON AN ORDER LAST NIGHT.
I'M GOING FIRST.


MASTER-SAMA...
I'VE BEEN SO GOOD... GIVE ME MY REWARD...

HOW DOES IT FEEL...
ALL OUR BODIES PUSHED AGAINST YOU?
Bounce
Ah...
Suck Suck
b-dmp
SO SOFT...
IT FEELS INCREDIBLE!
b-dmp
b-dmp
b-dmp
Twitch
NH...!
Lick Lick
MASTER-SAMA... YOUR HANDS ARE SO WARM.
HAAA...!
HAAAH...!

Lick
NHH...
WE'LL HOLD YOU UP, DON'T WORRY.
IT'S SO GOOD TO FEEL YOUR WEIGHT ON ME.
b-dmp
b-dmp
MORE, SHO-CHIN...
I WANT MORE, MASTER-SAMA!
M...
MASTER-SHI, Y-YOU PERVERT...!
Suck
Ah!
TWITCH
Ah!
Ahn!
AH... OH M...
Suck Kiss
THAT FEELS SO GOOD!
Shiver Shiver
Lick Lick
NHHH...NH!

I'M NOT HEAVY, AM I?
Twirl Twirl
NHHAA ...!

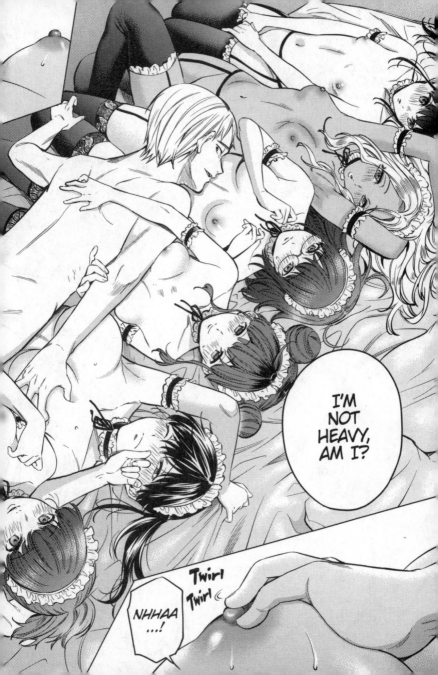

GO AHEAD AND ENJOY YOURSELF...

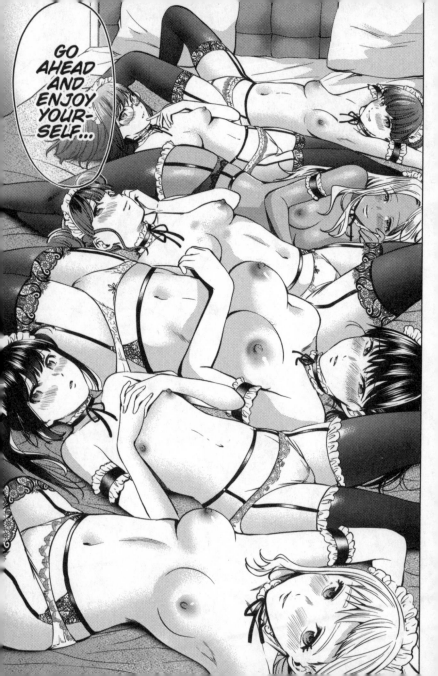

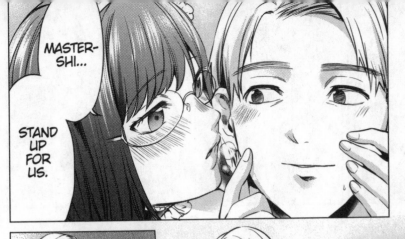

MASTER-SHI...

STAND UP FOR US.

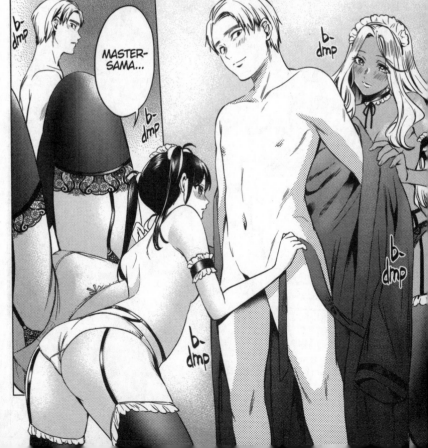

MASTER-SAMA...

b-dmp

b-dmp

b-dmp

b-dmp

WHAT A SIGHT TO BEHOLD...
Gulp...
WELL THEN, ENJOYYY! ★
b-dmp
b-dmp
b-dmp
b-dmp
b-dmp
COME HERE...
MASTER-SAMA...
I'VE MISSED YOU SO MUCH.
LET'S GET YOU ALL NICE AND CLEANED UP...
NHH...♥

SHO-CHIN ...
TODAY YOU'RE OUR MASTER-SAMA, *HMM?*
YOU CAN ORDER US TO DO WHATEVER YOU WANT.
I'LL TRY MY BEST TO SATISFY YOU, MASTER-SAMA.
SHO-YAN...
YOU'RE INTO THIS STUFF?
GETTING EXCITED AFTER SEEING US LIKE THIS. YOU TRULY ARE A SADISTIC MASS OF LEWD ENERGY, DOI-SHI.
RIKKA'S NEVER WORN *AAANYTHING* LIKE THIS BEFORE!
FEELS KINDA WEIRD.
M-
M-
MASTER-SAMA... PLEASE LOOK AFTER ME.

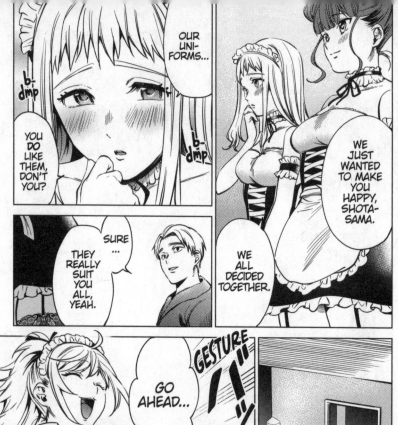

OUR UNI-FORMS...

b-dmp

YOU DO LIKE THEM, DON'T YOU?

b-dmp

WE JUST WANTED TO MAKE YOU HAPPY, SHOTA-SAMA.

SURE... THEY REALLY SUIT YOU ALL, YEAH.

WE ALL DECIDED TOGETHER.

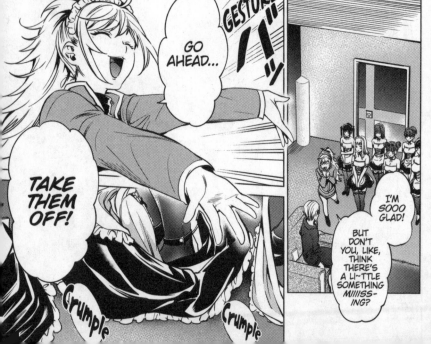

GO AHEAD...

GESTURE

TAKE THEM OFF!

Crumple

Crumple

I'M SOOO GLAD!

BUT DON'T YOU, LIKE, THINK THERE'S A LI~TTLE SOMETHING MIIIISS-ING?

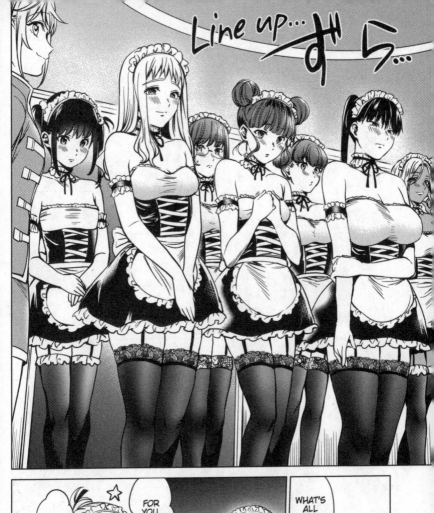

Line up... ゔ5...

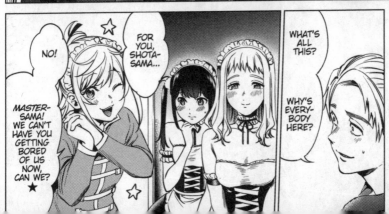

NO!

FOR YOU, SHOTA-SAMA...

MASTER-SAMA! WE CAN'T HAVE YOU GETTING BORED OF US NOW, CAN WE?

WHAT'S ALL THIS?

WHY'S EVERYBODY HERE?

INSIDE UW JAPAN BRANCH.
KNOCK KNOCK
COME IN.
The Prince
Peep
SHOTA-SAMAAA!
DO YOU HAVE A MOMENT?
!
TMP TMP
ぞろ
TMP, TMP
ぞろ

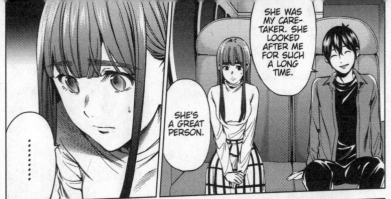

SHE WAS MY CARE-TAKER. SHE LOOKED AFTER ME FOR SUCH A LONG TIME.

SHE'S A GREAT PERSON.

..........

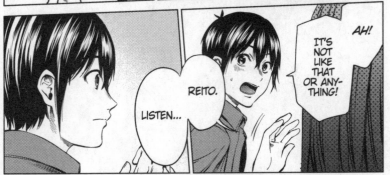

LISTEN...

REITO.

AH!

IT'S NOT LIKE THAT OR ANY-THING!

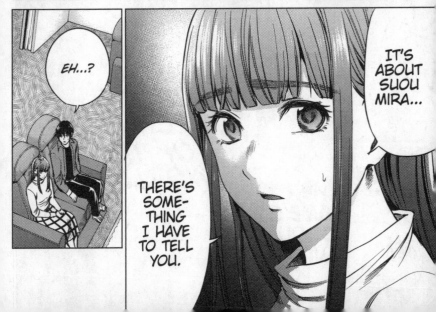

EH...?

IT'S ABOUT SUOU MIRA...

THERE'S SOME-THING I HAVE TO TELL YOU.

OH, COME TO THINK OF IT!
THERE'S SOMEBODY I WANT YOU TO MEET WHEN WE GET TO JAPAN.
WHO?
HER NAME'S SUOU MIRA.
!!
WILL DECIDE THE FATE OF THE WORLD...!

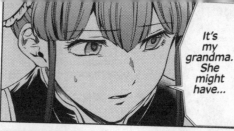

It's my grandma. She might have...

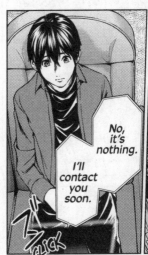

No, it's nothing.

I'll contact you soon.

ZZ CLICK

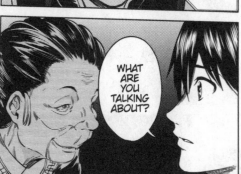

WHAT ARE YOU TALKING ABOUT?

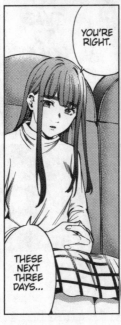

YOU'RE RIGHT.

THESE NEXT THREE DAYS...

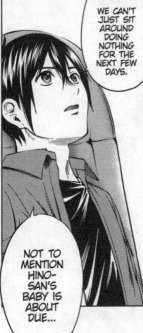

WE CAN'T JUST SIT AROUND DOING NOTHING FOR THE NEXT FEW DAYS.

NOT TO MENTION HINO-SAN'S BABY IS ABOUT DUE...

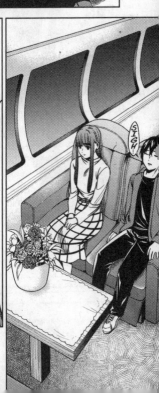

SIGH!

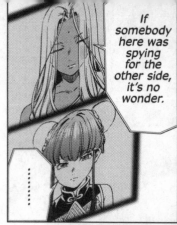

If somebody here was spying for the other side, it's no wonder.

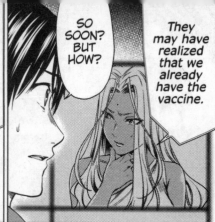

SO SOON? BUT HOW?

They may have realized that we already have the vaccine.

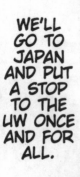

WE'LL GO TO JAPAN AND PUT A STOP TO THE UW ONCE AND FOR ALL.

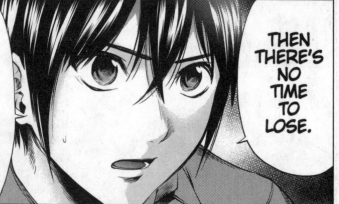

THEN THERE'S NO TIME TO LOSE.

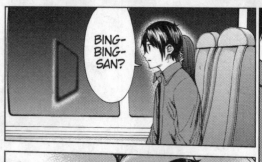

BING-BING-SAN?

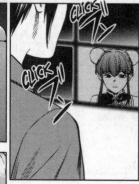

CLICK!!

CLICK!!

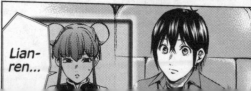

Lian-ren...

THE UW MIGHT TRY AND INTERFERE WITH YOUR EFFORTS.
PLEASE BE CAREFUL, EVERYONE.
WE NEED TO AWAKEN THE MEN IN SECRET AND GET THEM ON OUR SIDE.
THAT'LL CLEAR UP THIS BIG MISUNDERSTANDING UW PROPAGANDA HAS CREATED ABOUT LOSANIA, TOO!
I have an announcement to make.
WHAT'S THE MATTER?
I've heard reports from another leader's intelligence services...
They say the UW is preparing a missile launch.
!!!
WHO ARE THEY TARGETING?
I believe...
they intend to target Losania.

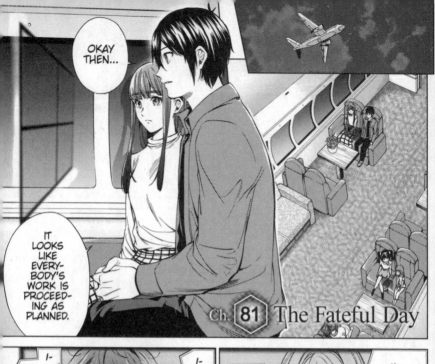

OKAY THEN...

IT LOOKS LIKE EVERY-BODY'S WORK IS PROCEED-ING AS PLANNED.

Ch. 81 The Fateful Day

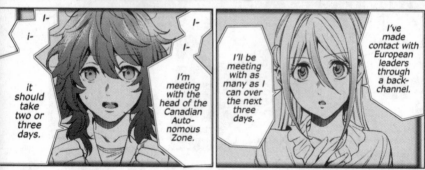

I- i- I- I-

it should take two or three days.

I'm meeting with the head of the Canadian Auto-nomous Zone.

I'll be meeting with as many as I can over the next three days.

I've made contact with European leaders through a back-channel.

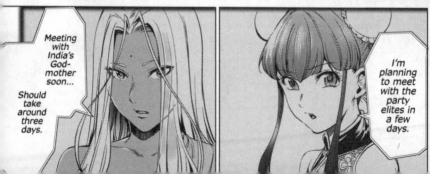

Meeting with India's God-mother soon...

Should take around three days.

I'm planning to meet with the party elites in a few days.

world's end harem

WHOOSH
I'M GOING TO KILL THE PATIENTS. EVERY LAST ONE OF THEM.

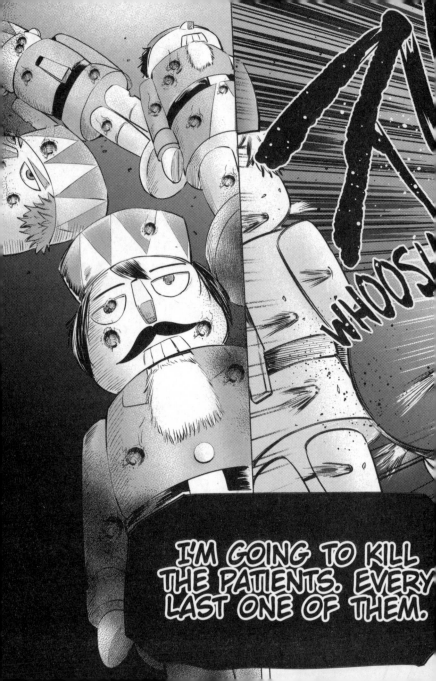

BANG
BANG
BANG
BANG
BANG
BANG
Rin...

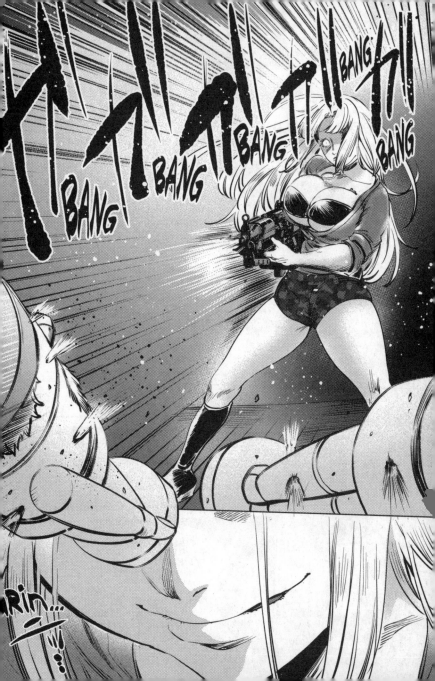

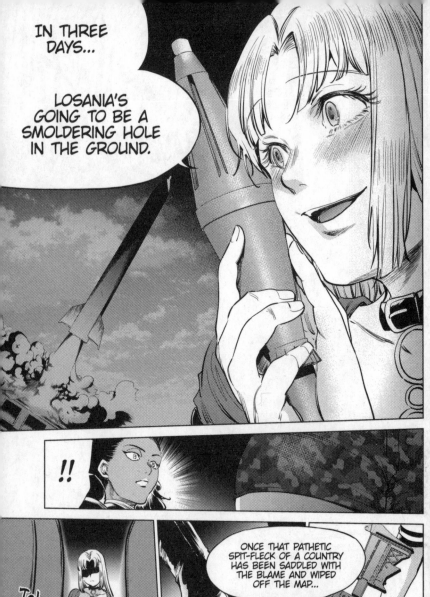

IN THREE DAYS...

LOSANIA'S GOING TO BE A SMOLDERING HOLE IN THE GROUND.

!!

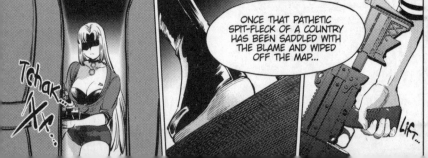

ONCE THAT PATHETIC SPIT-FLECK OF A COUNTRY HAS BEEN SADDLED WITH THE BLAME AND WIPED OFF THE MAP...

Tchak... Xr...

Lift...

CLICK
THE FINISHING TOUCHES ON OUR PLAN TO KILL *ALL* MEN.
WHIRR...
WE'LL TAKE THEM OUT ONE BY ONE.
CLACK...

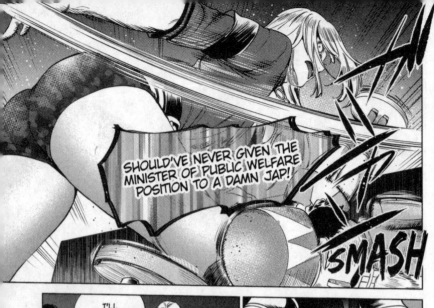

SHOULD'VE NEVER GIVEN THE MINISTER OF PUBLIC WELFARE POSITION TO A DAMN JAP!

SMASH

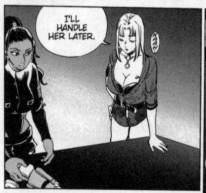

I'LL HANDLE HER LATER.

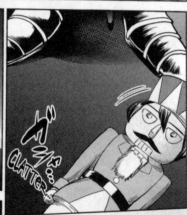

CLATTER...

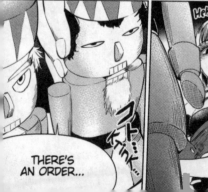

Heh!

THERE'S AN ORDER...

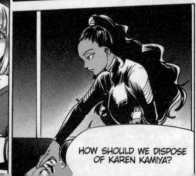

HOW SHOULD WE DISPOSE OF KAREN KAMIYA?

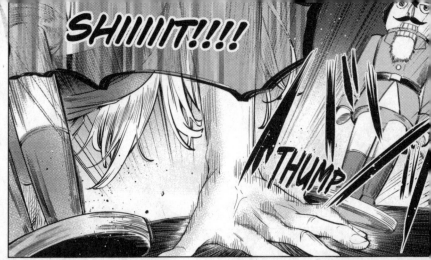

SHIIIIIT!!!!

THUMP

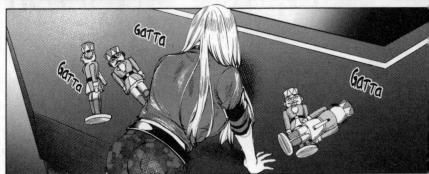

Gatta

Gatta

Gatta

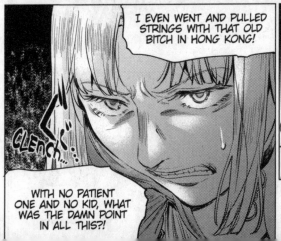

I EVEN WENT AND PULLED STRINGS WITH THAT OLD BITCH IN HONG KONG!

CLENCH...

WITH NO PATIENT ONE AND NO KID, WHAT WAS THE DAMN POINT IN ALL THIS?!

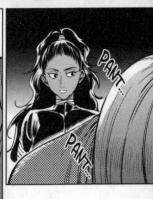

PANT...

PANT...

KYOJI-SA... MA...
LOOK AT ME...
I ONLY WANT YOU LOOKING AT ME...
SPURT
SPURT
Twitch
spasm
Nh! Mhn!
MNHAAAAH...!

Twitch Twitch
SPASM SPASM
NNNNNHH...!
I CAN'T WAIT...
HAAAH...
HAAAH...
I WANT YOU... KYOJI-SAMA...!
Ah!
NENE-KO-CHAN...!
THRUST THRUST
AAHHHHN...!
Ahn! Ah!

YOUR BACK...
Lick...
AHN...
NHH...!
AH...!
Twitch Twitch
YOUR ASS...
Squeeze
AHNN...!
YOUR BREASTS...
Rub
NNNHHH...!
Rub
AND...
BA-DMP
BA-DMP
HAA...!
BA-DMP
HAAAH!
BA-DMP
HAAAH!

I...
I ALWAYS WANTED YOU TO TOUCH ME!
B-DMP
Stroke...
B-DMP
NENEKO-CHAN, YOUR BODY...
B-DMP B-DMP
YOUR NECK...
Lick!...
NH...
YOUR LEGS...
Rub...
......!
IT'S SO BEAUTIFUL.

KYOJI... SAMA...
NENEKO-CHAN...
PRESS...
Kiss...
Kiss
Kiss
NH....

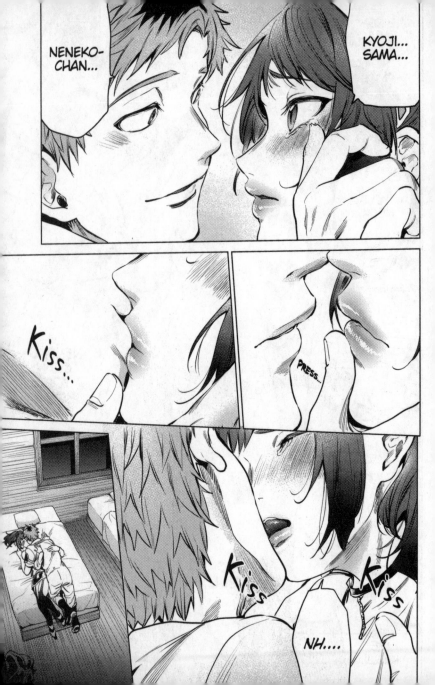

HUG
HINO-SAMA...
PLEASE, BE CAREFUL!
CALL ME KYOJI.

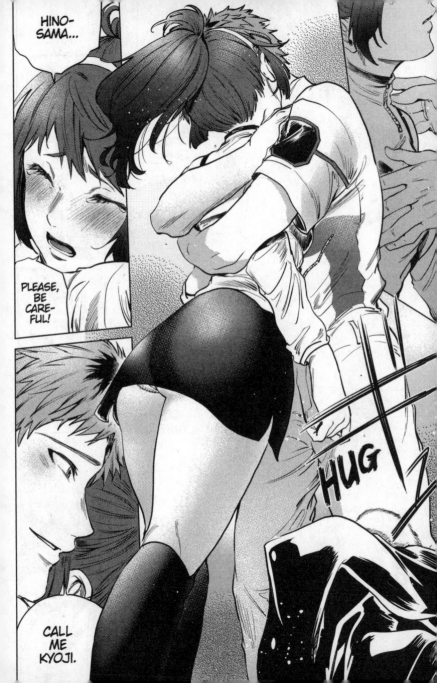

BUT NOW IT'S COME TO THIS...
AND YOU'RE *STILL* BEING KIND TO ME. YOU DON'T PLAY FAIR, DO YOU?
JUST FOR TONIGHT... WILL YOU NOT THINK OF ME AS YOUR CARE-TAKER...
BUT AS JUST ONE OF YOUR GIRLS?
HINO-SAMA...

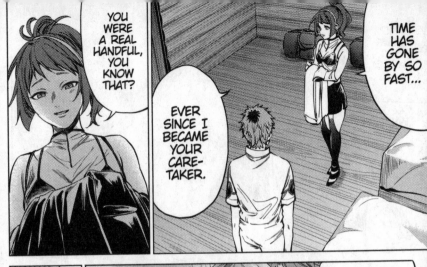

YOU WERE A REAL HANDFUL, YOU KNOW THAT?

EVER SINCE I BECAME YOUR CARE-TAKER.

TIME HAS GONE BY SO FAST...

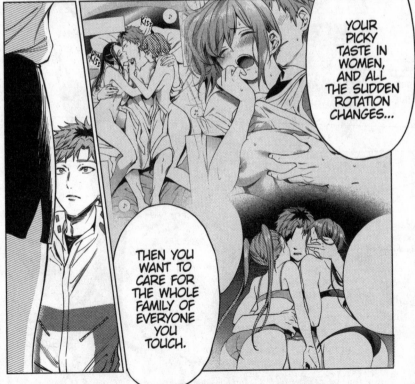

YOUR PICKY TASTE IN WOMEN, AND ALL THE SUDDEN ROTATION CHANGES...

THEN YOU WANT TO CARE FOR THE WHOLE FAMILY OF EVERYONE YOU TOUCH.

GET SOME SLEEP, HINO-SAMA.
I'LL BE HEADING BACK.
CAN'T YOU STAY HERE UNTIL WE JOIN UP WITH MIZUHARA-KUN AND THE OTHERS?
WHO KNOWS WHAT THOSE UW GUYS WILL DO TO YOU IF YOU GO BACK NOW...
I HAVE FAMILY BACK THERE.
I'LL BE FINE.
I DON'T KNOW WHERE YOU'RE GOING, EITHER.
THEY CAN QUESTION ME ALL THEY LIKE, AND I CAN NEVER GIVE YOU AWAY.
NENE-KO-CHAN...

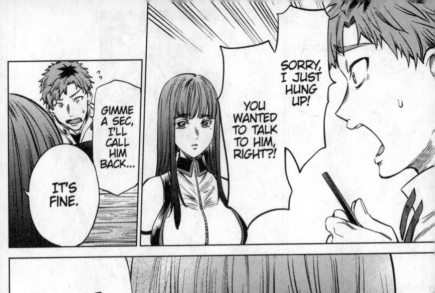

GIMME A SEC, I'LL CALL HIM BACK...

IT'S FINE.

YOU WANTED TO TALK TO HIM, RIGHT?!

SORRY, I JUST HUNG UP!

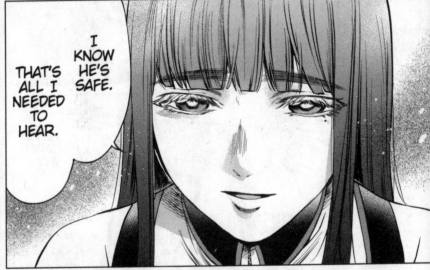

I KNOW HE'S SAFE.

THAT'S ALL I NEEDED TO HEAR.

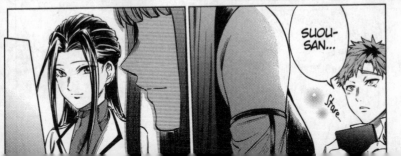

SUOU-SAN...

Stare...

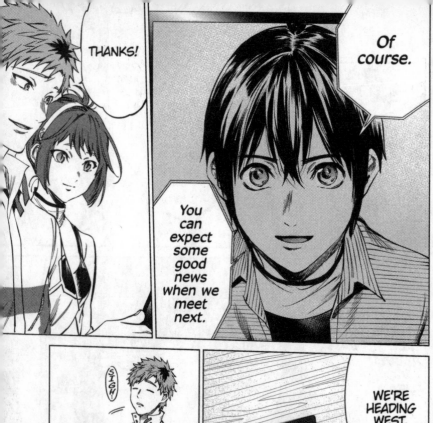

THANKS!

Of course.

You can expect some good news when we meet next.

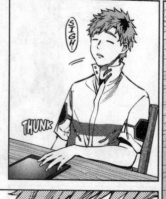

SIGH

THUNK

WE'RE HEADING WEST.

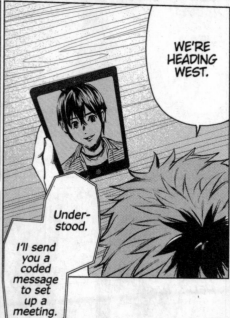

Under-stood.

I'll send you a coded message to set up a meeting.

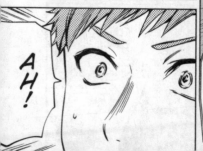

AH!

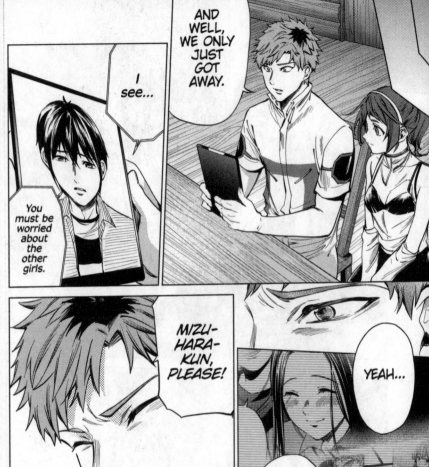

AND WELL, WE ONLY JUST GOT AWAY.

I see...

You must be worried about the other girls.

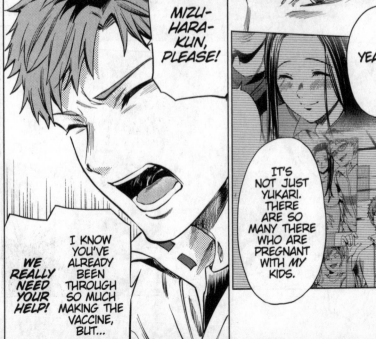

MIZU-HARA-KUN, PLEASE!

I KNOW YOU'VE ALREADY BEEN THROUGH SO MUCH MAKING THE VACCINE, BUT...

WE REALLY NEED YOUR HELP!

YEAH...

IT'S NOT JUST YUKARI. THERE ARE SO MANY THERE WHO ARE PREGNANT WITH MY KIDS.

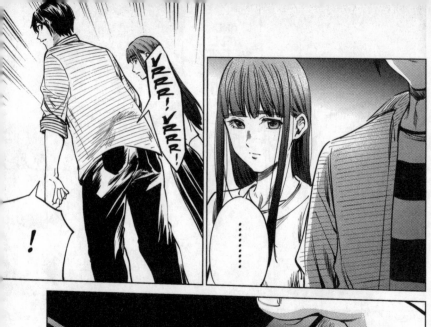

VRR! VRR!

!

. . . . . . . . .

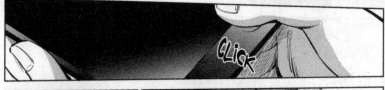

CLICK

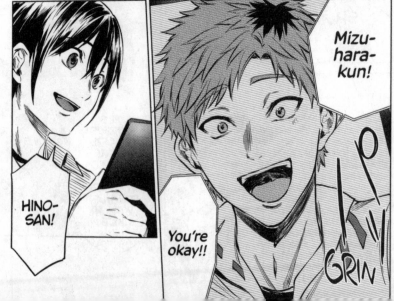

HINO-
SAN!

Mizu-
hara-
kun!

You're
okay!!

GRIN

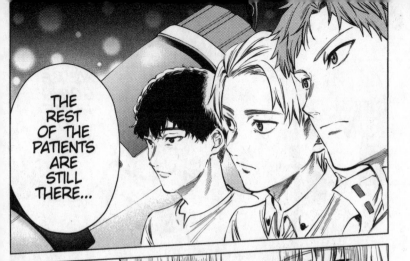

THE REST OF THE PATIENTS ARE STILL THERE...

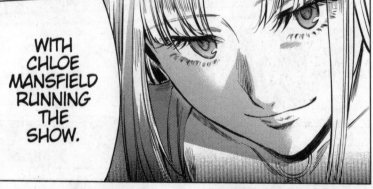

WITH CHLOE MANSFIELD RUNNING THE SHOW.

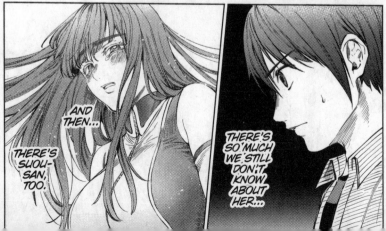

AND THEN...

THERE'S SHOU-SAN, TOO.

THERE'S SO MUCH WE STILL DON'T KNOW ABOUT HER...

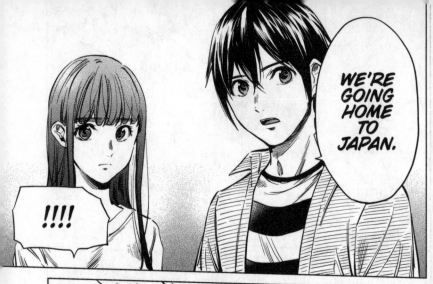

WE'RE GOING HOME TO JAPAN.

!!!!

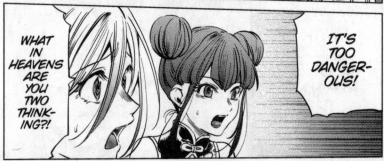

WHAT IN HEAVENS ARE YOU TWO THINK-ING?!

IT'S TOO DANGER-OUS!

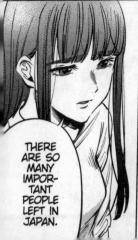

THERE ARE SO MANY IMPOR-TANT PEOPLE LEFT IN JAPAN.

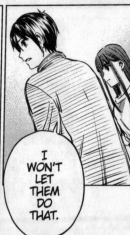

I WON'T LET THEM DO THAT.

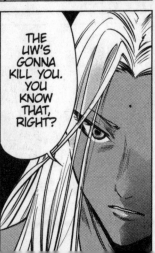

THE UW'S GONNA KILL YOU. YOU KNOW THAT, RIGHT?

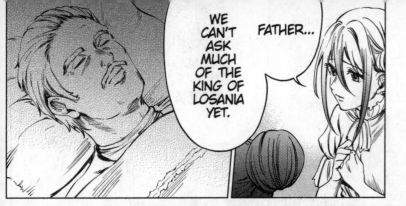

FATHER... WE CAN'T ASK MUCH OF THE KING OF LOSANIA YET.

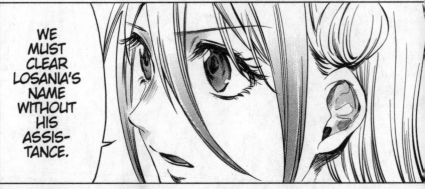

WE MUST CLEAR LOSANIA'S NAME WITHOUT HIS ASSISTANCE.

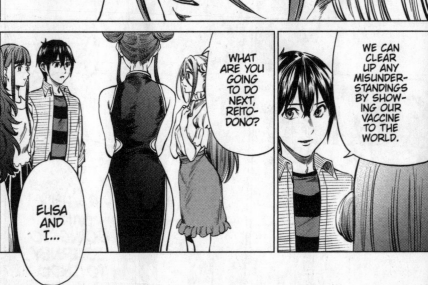

WHAT ARE YOU GOING TO DO NEXT, REITO-DONO?

WE CAN CLEAR UP ANY MISUNDERSTANDINGS BY SHOWING OUR VACCINE TO THE WORLD.

ELISA AND I...

I THINK IT'S ONLY A MATTER OF TIME BEFORE THE UW FIND US HERE.
WE'LL BE AT LESS RISK OF GETTING CAUGHT IF WE ALL SPLIT UP.
TRY TO SPREAD THE VACCINE AS FAR AS YOU CAN. FIND A WAY TO PRODUCE MORE OF IT.
AND MARI-CHAN'S GOING TO CANADA.
RAGINI-SAN'S GOING TO JOURNEY TO INDIA.

BINGBING-SAN WILL TRAVEL TO CHINA.
PRINCESS ANA WILL GO TO EUROPE.
THEN IT'S SETTLED.

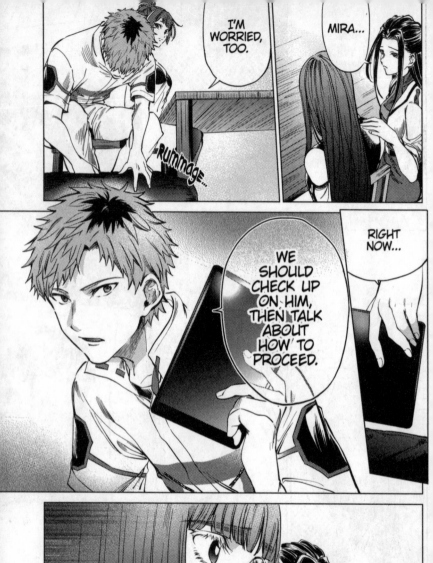

I'M WORRIED, TOO.

MIRA...

Rummage...

WE SHOULD CHECK UP ON HIM, THEN TALK ABOUT HOW TO PROCEED.

RIGHT NOW...

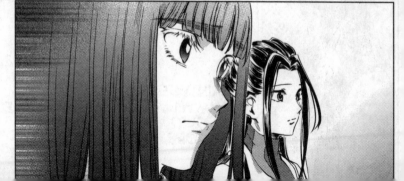

……
SUOU-SAN...
THAT'S YOUR NAME, ISN'T IT?
YES.
ARE YOU WORRIED...
ABOUT MIZU-HARA-KUN?
!
condition critical.
CLENCH
……
nod...

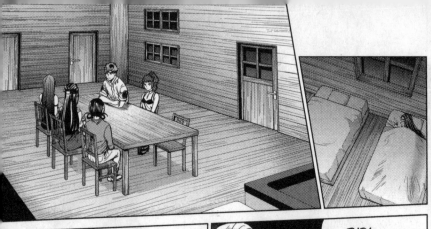

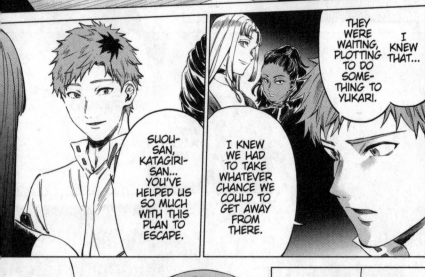

SUOU-SAN, KATAGIRI-SAN... YOU'VE HELPED US SO MUCH WITH THIS PLAN TO ESCAPE.

I KNEW WE HAD TO TAKE WHATEVER CHANCE WE COULD TO GET AWAY FROM THERE.

THEY WERE WAITING, PLOTTING TO DO SOMETHING TO YUKARI.

I KNEW THAT...

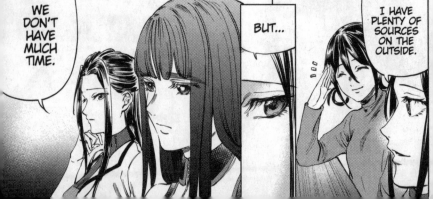

WE DON'T HAVE MUCH TIME.

BUT...

I HAVE PLENTY OF SOURCES ON THE OUTSIDE.

CREAK...
COME IN.
!
ISURUGI-SAN! HINO-SAN!
nod
Phew!
SO THE UW AREN'T ON OUR TAIL YET...

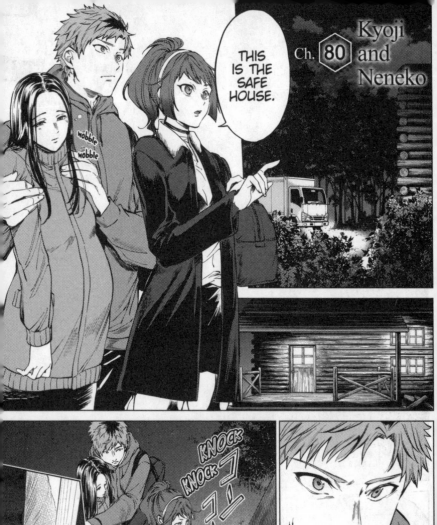

THIS IS THE SAFE HOUSE.

Ch. **80** Kyoji and Neneko

wobble wobble

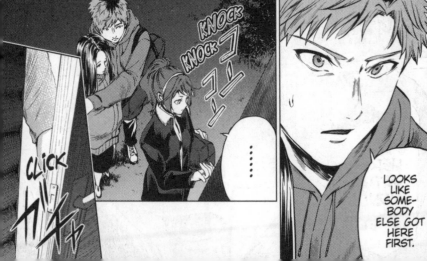

KNOCK KNOCK

CLICK

. . . . .

LOOKS LIKE SOMEBODY ELSE GOT HERE FIRST.

KYO-CHAN... I'M SO SCARED!
RATTLE
Bump
RATTLE
DON'T WORRY.
I'M HERE WITH YOU!

VROOOM
......
Bump
CLATTER
CLATTER

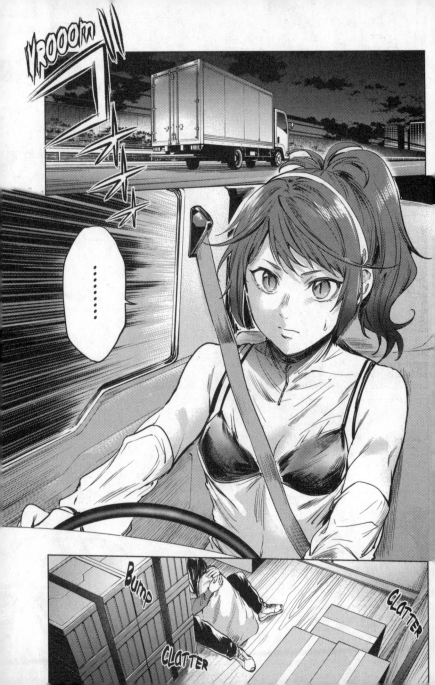

UM...
PROMISE YOU WON'T GET MAD?
WHAT IS IT?
GET TO THE POINT ALREADY!
Rage
Rage
Wahhh!
IT'S REGARDING THOSE TWO YOU'RE TALKING ABOUT, SEE...
HAS THE BABY BEEN BORN?
NOT EXACTLY...
Wink
LOOKS LIKE THEY'VE GONE AND ESCAPED. ★
??!!

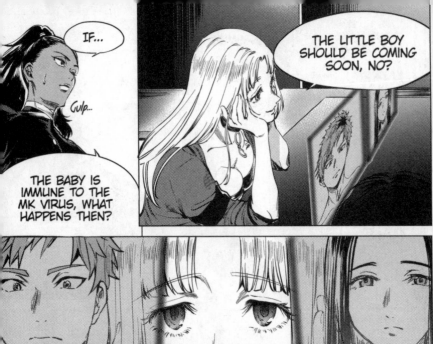

IF...

Gulp...

THE LITTLE BOY SHOULD BE COMING SOON, NO?

THE BABY IS IMMUNE TO THE MK VIRUS, WHAT HAPPENS THEN?

SOMETHING TERRIBLY SAD, I'M AFRAID.

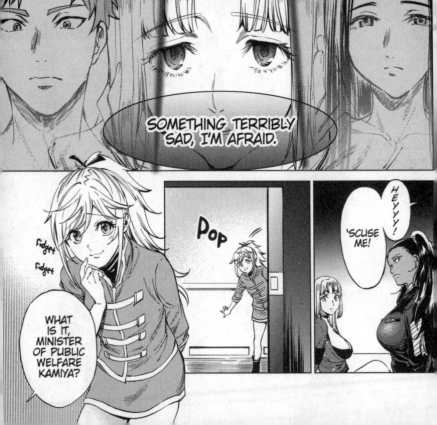

fidget

fidget

WHAT IS IT, MINISTER OF PUBLIC WELFARE KAMIYA?

Pop

'SCUSE ME!

HEYYY!

UW JAPAN BRANCH.
ALL IS PROCEEDING AS PLANNED.
THE MOTHERS ARE GONNA BE HAPPY BACK HOME.
WHO WOULD'VE THOUGHT THEY'D ACTUALLY CREATE A VACCINE...
*I'M* SHOCKED, TO SAY THE LEAST.
ENOUGH, ENOUGH. WE'RE HANDLING IT.
SWIPE
MORE IMPORTANTLY...
KYOJI HINO...
NO.
YUKARI KUSAKABE.

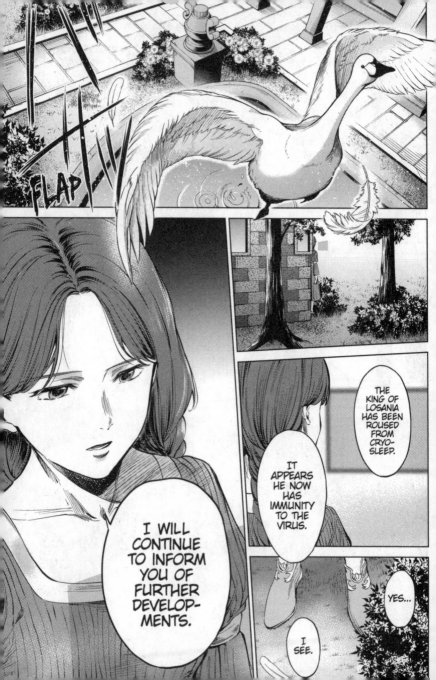

FLAP

THE KING OF LOSANIA HAS BEEN ROUSED FROM CRYO-SLEEP.

IT APPEARS HE NOW HAS IMMUNITY TO THE VIRUS.

I WILL CONTINUE TO INFORM YOU OF FURTHER DEVELOPMENTS.

YES...

I SEE.

RAGINI-SAN!
YOU'RE AN AMAZING SCIENTIST. YOU REALLY ARE!
Smirk
REITO...
ELISA, THIS GOES FOR YOU TOO.
YOU DID THIS. NOT ME.
I'M SO HAPPY ...
WE FINALLY DID IT!

VITAL SIGNS ALL CHECK OUT.
NO INTER-NAL BLEED-ING.
FATHER ...!
THAT MEANS ...
THE VACCINE'S WORKING.
HE'S DEVELOPED AN IMMUNE RESPONSE TO THE VIRUS, JUST LIKE YOU.
WE DID IT!!

!!
FATHER ...!!
......
FATHER!
FATHER CAN YOU HEAR ME?!
A...
ANA-STASIA...?

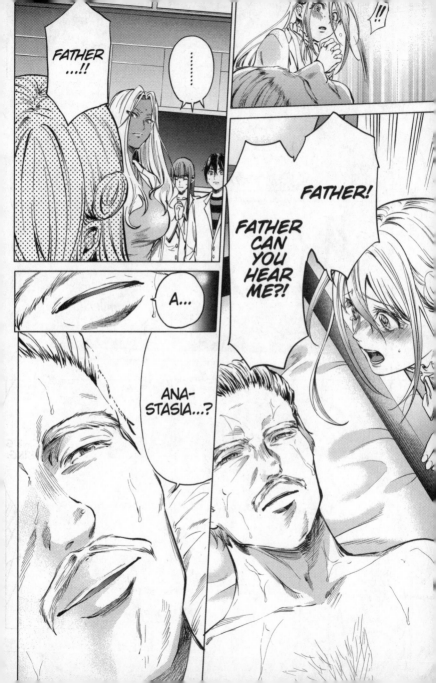

Resuscitating patient.
......!
Resuscitating patient.
Resuscitation complete.
Resuscitation complete.
ウィィ…ン
Vwoosh...
......

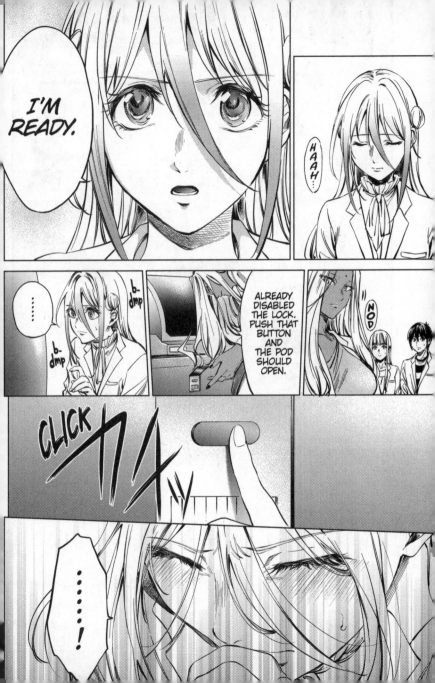

I'M READY.

HAAH...

. . . . .

b-dmp

b-dmp

ALREADY DISABLED THE LOCK. PUSH THAT BUTTON AND THE POD SHOULD OPEN.

NOD

CLICK

. . . . . . !

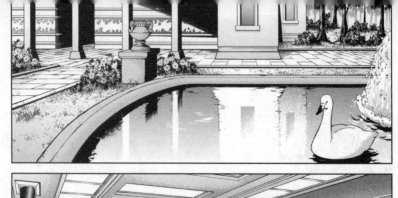

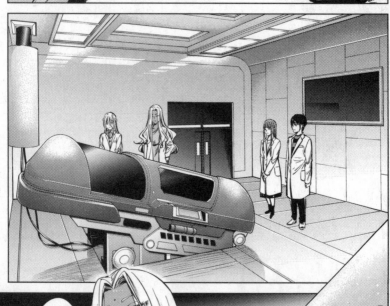

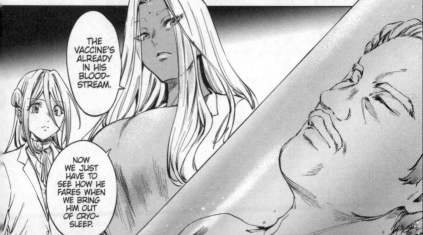

THE VACCINE'S ALREADY IN HIS BLOOD-STREAM.

NOW WE JUST HAVE TO SEE HOW HE FARES WHEN WE BRING HIM OUT OF CRYO-SLEEP.

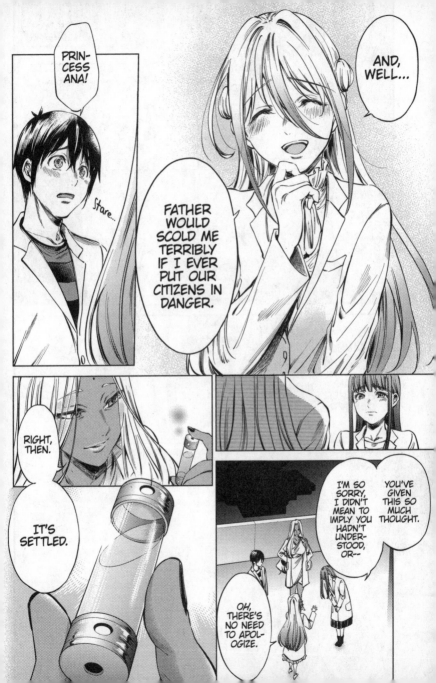

PRIN-CESS ANA!

AND, WELL...

Stare...

FATHER WOULD SCOLD ME TERRIBLY IF I EVER PUT OUR CITIZENS IN DANGER.

RIGHT, THEN.

IT'S SETTLED.

I'M SO SORRY, I DIDN'T MEAN TO IMPLY YOU HADN'T UNDER-STOOD, OR--

YOU'VE GIVEN THIS SO MUCH THOUGHT.

OH, THERE'S NO NEED TO APOLO-GIZE.

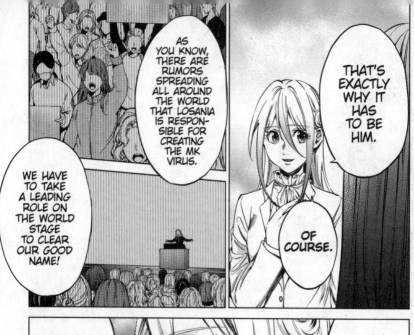

AS YOU KNOW, THERE ARE RUMORS SPREADING ALL AROUND THE WORLD THAT LOSANIA IS RESPONSIBLE FOR CREATING THE MK VIRUS.

THAT'S EXACTLY WHY IT HAS TO BE HIM.

WE HAVE TO TAKE A LEADING ROLE ON THE WORLD STAGE TO CLEAR OUR GOOD NAME!

OF COURSE.

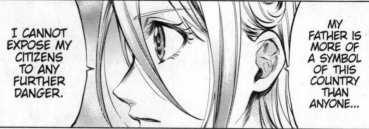

I CANNOT EXPOSE MY CITIZENS TO ANY FURTHER DANGER.

MY FATHER IS MORE OF A SYMBOL OF THIS COUNTRY THAN ANYONE...

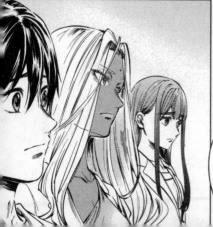

I ALSO HAVE A BROTHER.

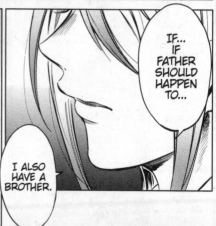

IF... IF FATHER SHOULD HAPPEN TO...

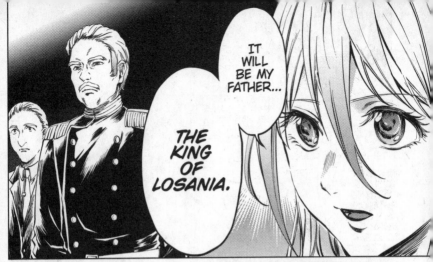

IT WILL BE MY FATHER...

THE KING OF LOSANIA.

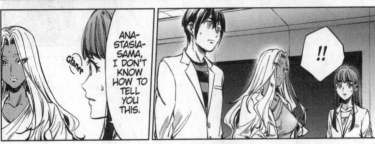

ANA-STASIA-SAMA, I DON'T KNOW HOW TO TELL YOU THIS.

Glance

!!

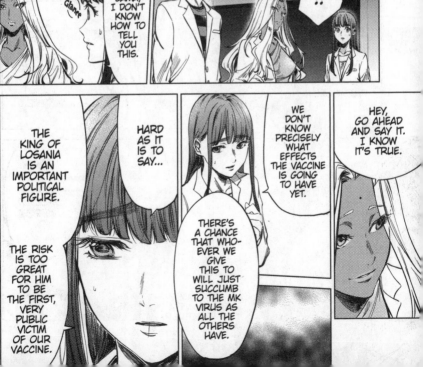

THE KING OF LOSANIA IS AN IMPORTANT POLITICAL FIGURE.

THE RISK IS TOO GREAT FOR HIM TO BE THE FIRST, VERY PUBLIC VICTIM OF OUR VACCINE.

HARD AS IT IS TO SAY...

WE DON'T KNOW PRECISELY WHAT EFFECTS THE VACCINE IS GOING TO HAVE YET.

THERE'S A CHANCE THAT WHO-EVER WE GIVE THIS TO WILL JUST SUCCUMB TO THE MK VIRUS AS ALL THE OTHERS HAVE.

HEY, GO AHEAD AND SAY IT. I KNOW IT'S TRUE.

WE'VE GOT A VACCINE.
JUST NEED TO FIGURE OUT HOW TO MANU-FACTURE IT IN BULK.
BUT FIRST... THERE'S ANOTHER BIG STEP WE NEED TO TAKE.
I KNOW...
WE HAVE TO TEST THE VACCINE'S EFFECTIVE-NESS.
WHO DO WE USE IT ON FIRST?
TIGHTEN...
I HAVE ALREADY DECIDED THAT MUCH.

Tmp...
...
RAGINI-SAN!
PRO-FESSOR SHIN!
SO, UM... HOW DID IT GO?
stare...
......
lift
WE DID IT.
YES ...!

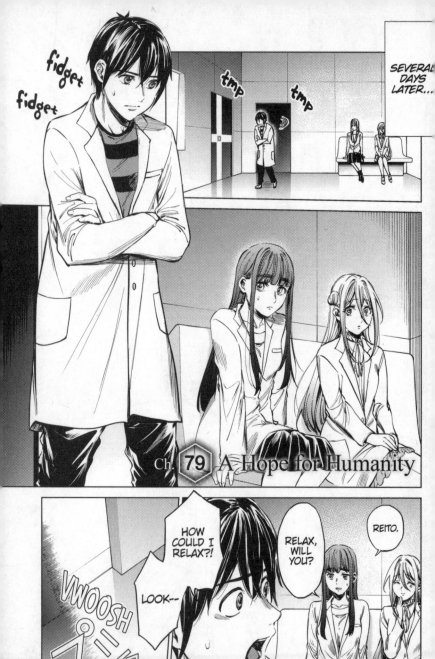

SEVERAL DAYS LATER...

fidget
fidget

tmp

tmp

Ch. 79 A Hope for Humanity

HOW COULD I RELAX?!

LOOK--

VWOOSH

RELAX, WILL YOU?

REITO.

world's end harem

FINALLY...
WE CAN MAKE A VACCINE...!

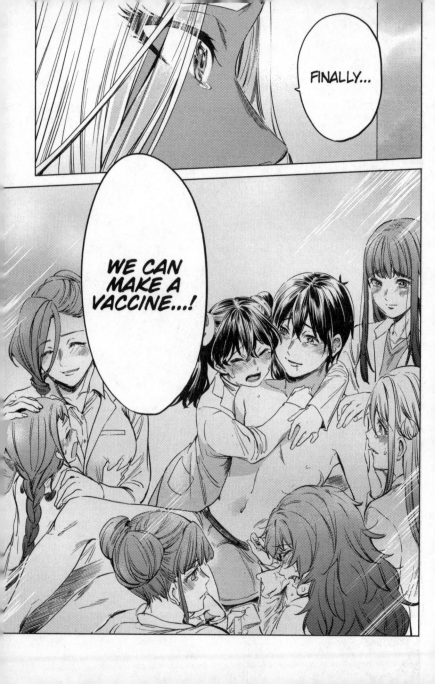

REITO...!

HIS WILL TO STAY ALIVE BEAT OUT THE VIRUS!

WE'VE JUST COMPLETED A FULL SCAN.

THE MICRO-BOTS HAVE ALSO HARVESTED THE NECESSARY PROTEINS.

??!!
R...
REITO ...?!
HAAAH...
HAAAH...
Wipe
TH...
THE BLEEDING'S STOPPED...

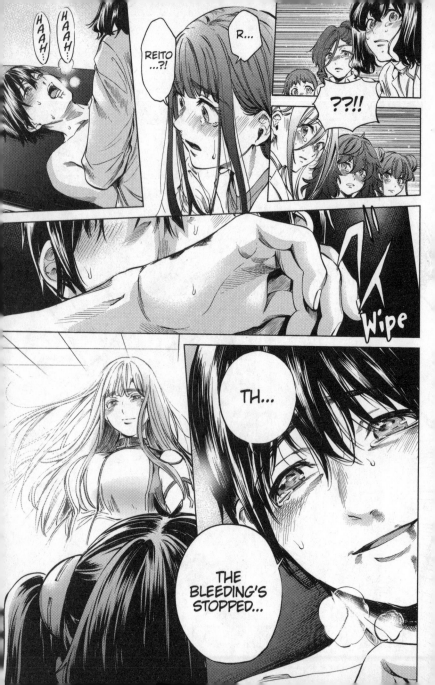

URRAAAAAAAAGGHH!!
SPASM

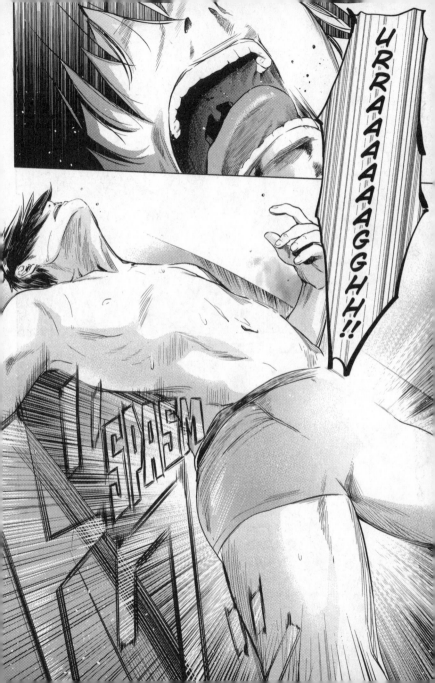

PRO-FESSOR SHIN...
COME TAKE A LOOK AT THIS!
!!
THIS IS...
IT CAN'T BE ...!
YES...
THE MK VIRUS ...
TWITCH
IT'S RAPIDLY DISAP-PEAR-ING...!

I WANT TO LIVE...!

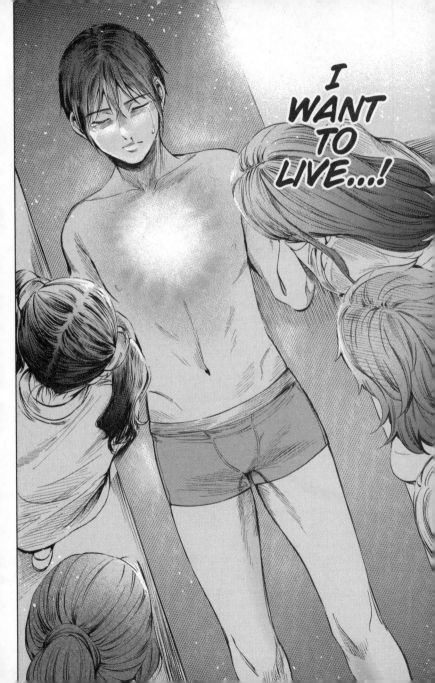

ELISA...
SUOU-SAN...
EVERY-ONE...
I...
TEAR...!!
I'M NOT LETTING GO YET.

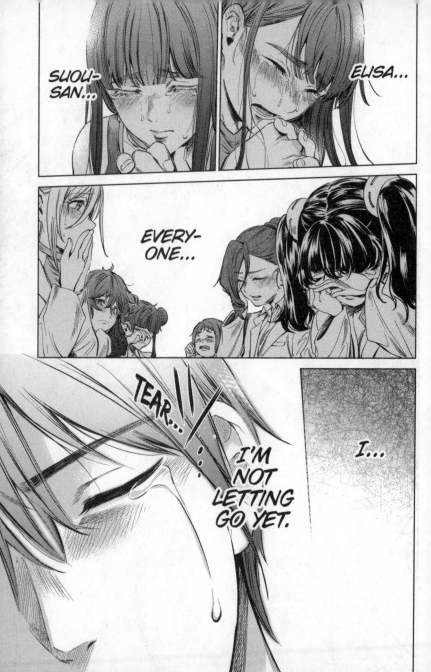

REITO-SAMA...
PLEASE... LIVE...!
REITO!
HOLD ON!

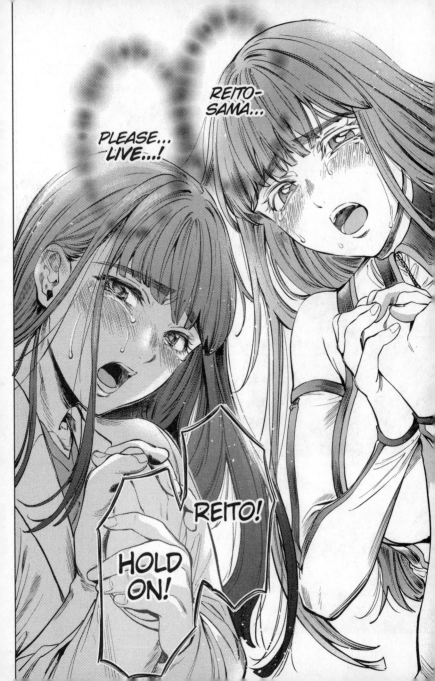

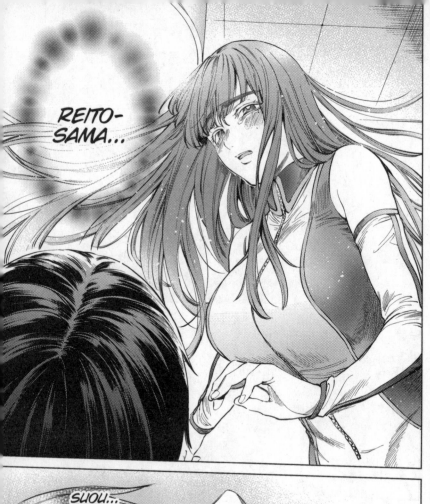

REITO-
SAMA...

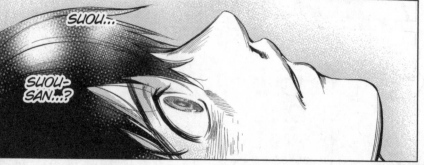

SUOU...

SUOU-
SAN...?

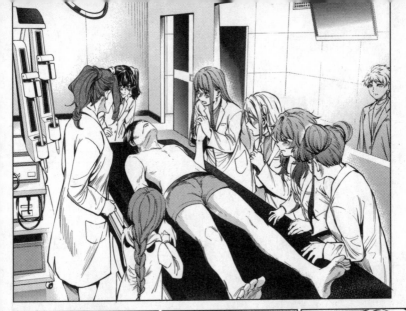

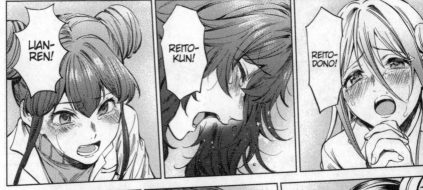

LIAN-
REN!

REITO-
KUN!

REITO-
DONO!

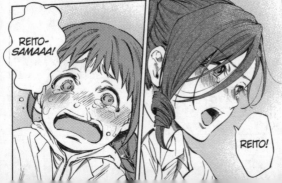

REITO-
SAMAAA!

REITO!

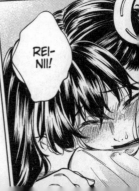

REI-
NII!

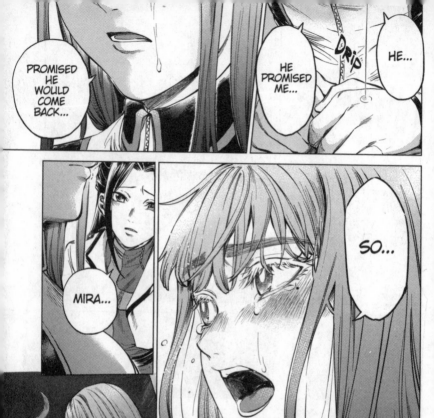

PROMISED HE WOULD COME BACK...

HE PROMISED ME...

DRIP

HE...

MIRA...

SO...

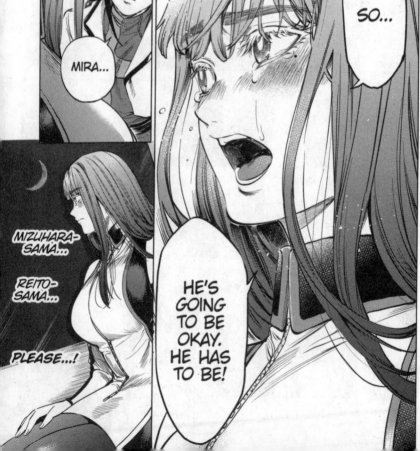

MIZUHARA-SAMA...

REITO-SAMA...

PLEASE...!

HE'S GOING TO BE OKAY. HE HAS TO BE!

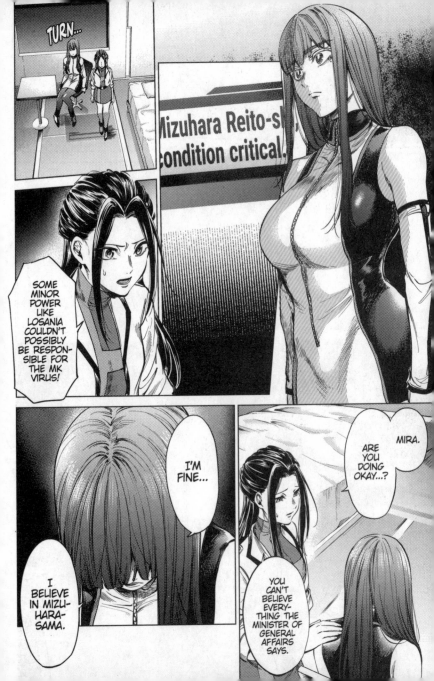

TURN...

Mizuhara Reito-sh~
~ondition critical.

SOME MINOR POWER LIKE LOSANIA COULDN'T POSSIBLY BE RESPONSIBLE FOR THE MK VIRUS!

I'M FINE...

I BELIEVE IN MIZU- HARA- SAMA.

MIRA.

ARE YOU DOING OKAY...?

YOU CAN'T BELIEVE EVERY- THING THE MINISTER OF GENERAL AFFAIRS SAYS.

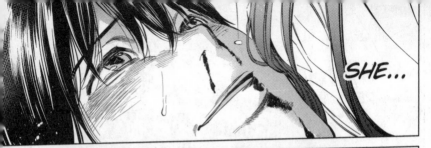

SHE...

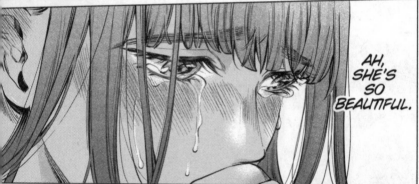

AH, SHE'S SO BEAUTIFUL.

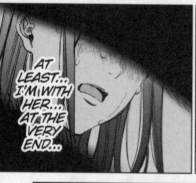

AT LEAST... I'M WITH HER... AT THE VERY END...

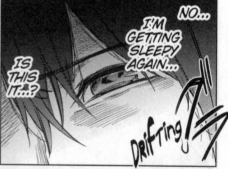

IS THIS IT...?

NO... I'M GETTING SLEEPY AGAIN...

Drifting

DIDN'T I...

HAVE ONE MORE PROMISE TO KEEP...?

SQUEEZE
DON'T YOU REMEMBER?!
I'LL WAIT FOR YOU...
NO MATTER HOW LONG IT TAKES!!

FINE...
I'M BETTER NOW.
Sob...
......
OH...
I... I'M GOING TO DIE, AREN'T I...?
YOU WON'T...
YOU AREN'T GOING TO DIE!
WE'LL JUST PUT YOU BACK INTO CRYO-SLEEP!
HEY...
HOW LONG ARE YOU GOING TO PUT ME ON ICE FOR THIS TIME?

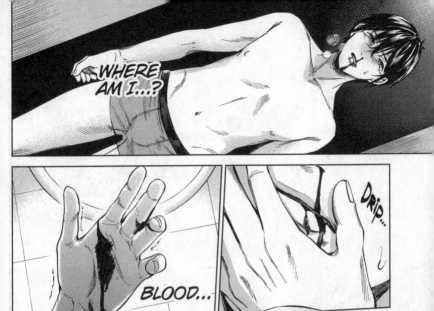

WHERE AM I...?

BLOOD...

DRIP...

ELISA...

REITO!

HOW'S YOUR FEVER?

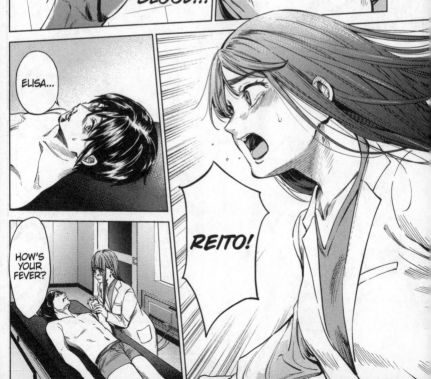

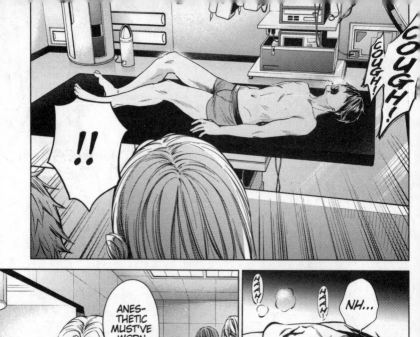

COUGH! COUGH! COUGH!

!!

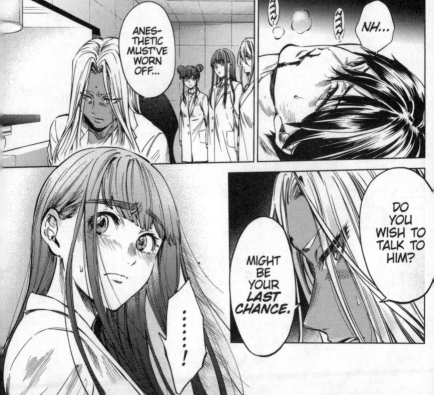

ANES- THETIC MUST'VE WORN OFF...

HAH! HAH! HAH! NH...

DO YOU WISH TO TALK TO HIM?

MIGHT BE YOUR *LAST* CHANCE.

......!

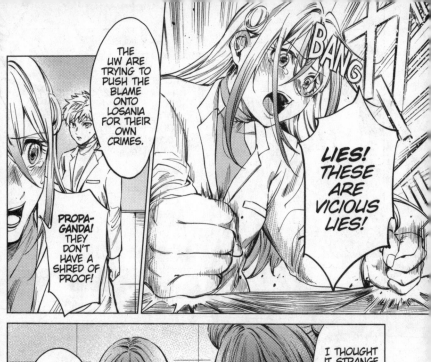

THE UW ARE TRYING TO PUSH THE BLAME ONTO LOSANIA FOR THEIR OWN CRIMES.

PROPA- GANDA! THEY DON'T HAVE A SHRED OF PROOF!

LIES! THESE ARE VICIOUS LIES!

BANG

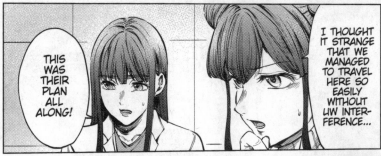

THIS WAS THEIR PLAN ALL ALONG!

I THOUGHT IT STRANGE THAT WE MANAGED TO TRAVEL HERE SO EASILY WITHOUT UW INTER- FERENCE...

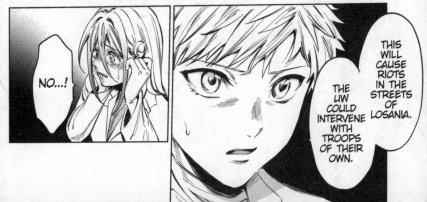

NO...!

THIS WILL CAUSE RIOTS IN THE STREETS OF LOSANIA.

THE UW COULD INTERVENE WITH TROOPS OF THEIR OWN.

They kidnapped Mizuhara Reito-shi...
and it's currently believed that he is fighting for his life after being injected with a highly concentrated dose of the MK Virus.
What reasons the Kingdom of Losania had for carrying out these plans are still unclear, but it appears they have been underway prior to the 2040 outbreak.
Smirk
........

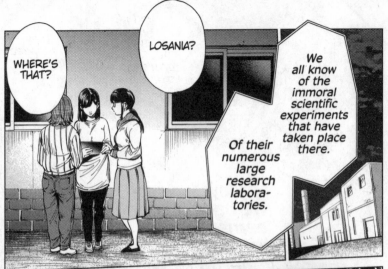

LOSANIA?

WHERE'S THAT?

We all know of the immoral scientific experiments that have taken place there.

Of their numerous large research laboratories.

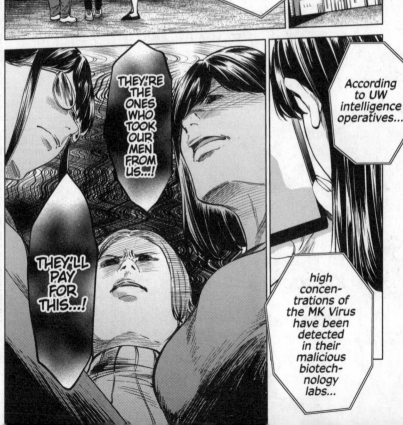

THEY'RE THE ONES WHO TOOK OUR MEN FROM US...!

THEY'LL PAY FOR THIS...!

According to UW intelligence operatives...

high concentrations of the MK Virus have been detected in their malicious biotechnology labs...

Citizens of the world...
today, we have learned a hard and important truth.
The identity of those responsible for first spreading the MK virus five years ago...
The source of this plague...
is the Kingdom of Losania!
??!!

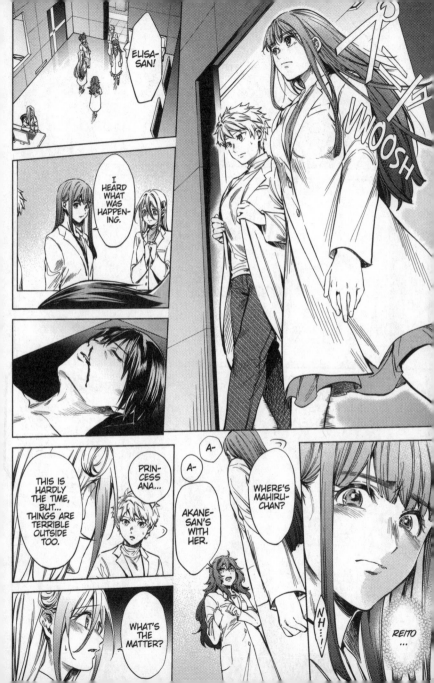

ELISA-SAN!

I HEARD WHAT WAS HAPPEN-ING.

THIS IS HARDLY THE TIME, BUT... THINGS ARE TERRIBLE OUTSIDE TOO.

PRIN-CESS ANA...

A-

A-

AKANE-SAN'S WITH HER.

WHERE'S MAHIRU-CHAN?

WHAT'S THE MATTER?

NH...!

REITO...

Y- Y-
YOU CAN'T!
I ONLY CAME TO SAY GOOD-BYE.
SEE YOU.
turn
NH...!
HOW CAN YOU JUST THROW REITO-DONO AWAY LIKE THIS?!
WHAT ELSE AM I SUP-POSED TO DO?!
I CAN'T STAY HERE.
I CAN'T WATCH LIANREN DIE!
BING-BING-SAN...

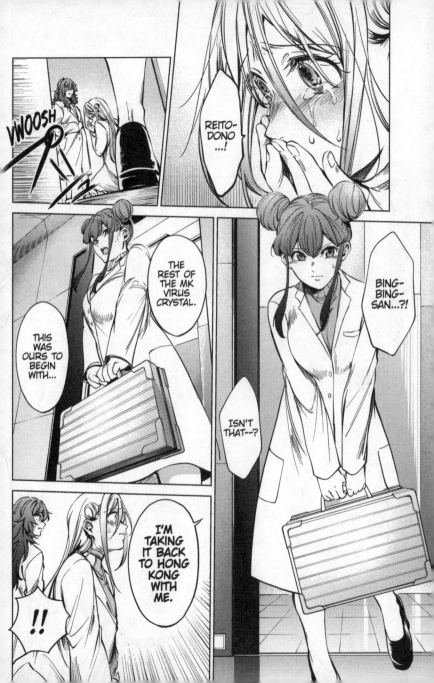

VWOOSH

REITO-DONO...!

THE REST OF THE MK VIRUS CRYSTAL.

THIS WAS OURS TO BEGIN WITH...

BING-BING-SAN...?!

ISN'T THAT--?

I'M TAKING IT BACK TO HONG KONG WITH ME.

!!

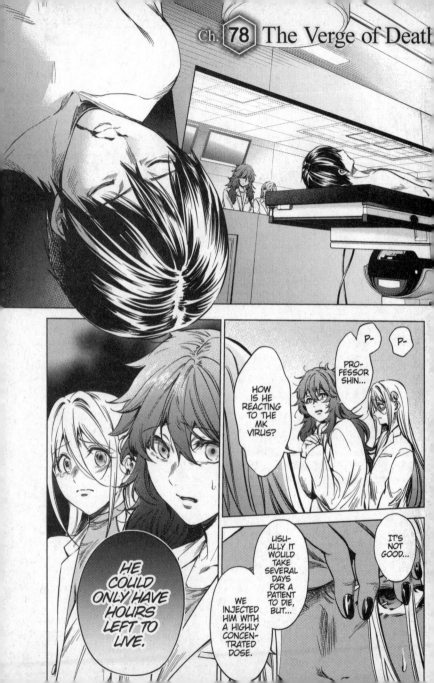

HOW IS HE REACTING TO THE MK VIRUS?

P-

P-

PRO-FESSOR SHIN...

IT'S NOT GOOD...

USU-ALLY IT WOULD TAKE SEVERAL DAYS FOR A PATIENT TO DIE, BUT...

WE INJECTED HIM WITH A HIGHLY CONCEN-TRATED DOSE.

HE COULD ONLY HAVE HOURS LEFT TO LIVE.

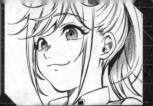

## Doi Shota

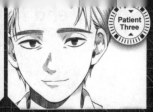

**Patient Three**

Shota's personal caretaker.
Aims to acquire power within the UW;
collaborating with Shota in order to do so.

A high school student and the third
man to be awakened. Targeted by
bullies before he entered cryosleep.
Infatuated with his homeroom teacher,
Hanyu Yuzuki, whom he affectionately
calls Yuzu-sensei.

## Isurugi Neneko

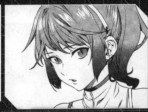

## Hino Kyoji

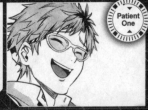

**Patient One**

Kyoji's personal caretaker.
Is attempting to protect Kyoji from
the UW Headquarters' higher-ups.

The first man to be awakened. Actively
engaged in the mating process. Was
turned down by Mahiru.

### Chloe Mansfield

A high-ranking member of UW Headquarters.
Directs the organization's military forces.
Temporarily overseeing the Japan Branch.

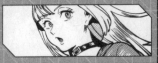

## The Events of *World's End Harem* Thus Far  STORY

In the year 2040, a university student named Reito contracts a fatal condition known as "cellular
sclerosis." He enters cryosleep to await the development of a cure, promising to one day reunite
with the girl he loves: his childhood friend, Elisa. However, when Reito awakens five years later,
he finds the world completely changed. A pandemic caused by the MK Virus ("Male Killer Virus")
has eliminated at least 99.9% of the male population, leaving behind a planet of only women.

After finding out about the changes taking place within Elisa's body, Reito visits her alone to find out
the truth—that she is unable to have children. As Elisa speaks about her past, Reito sees how much
she had been keeping inside, and the two finally spend a night together to express their feelings for
each other.

At UW Japan Branch, the due date for Yukari and Kyoji's child is getting closer, and all are shocked
by Chloe's revelation that Mira is Elisa's clone... Professor Shin comes rushing into the lab to see
Reito, in the midst of attempting to create a vaccine for the MK Virus, spitting up blood. Has he

# world's end harem CHARACTERS

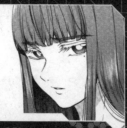

## Suou Mira

Reito's former personal caretaker. Has an appearance quite similar to that of Elisa and a mysterious past. Currently operating apart from Reito.

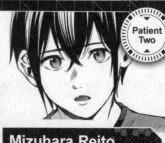

Patient Two

## Mizuhara Reito

A medical student and the second man to be awakened. Has strong feelings for his childhood friend, Elisa, and is avoidant of the mating process.

One of Reito's new personal caretakers. Dislikes men and has a past with Mira. Currently operating apart from Reito.

**Katagiri Rea**

One of Reito's new personal caretakers. A researcher specializing in virology. Tends to forget to wear clothes.

**Kuroda Maria**

Reito's personal bodyguard. Normally has a sweet temperament, but quickly shifts into high gear when there's work to be done.

**Sui**

Reito's personal nurse. Loves to drink. Pounces on Reito at every opportunity.

**Ryuzoji Akane**

Reito's little sister. Extremely attached to her brother. Visits the refugee districts.

**Mizuhara Mahiru**

Reito's childhood friend. A high-ranking member of Izanami. Intent on developing a cure for the MK Virus.

**Tachibana Elisa**

A mysterious, well-connected woman who rescued Reito and his caretakers from danger in Hong Kong. Her whole body smells like peaches.

**Bingbing**

The eccentric princess of the Kingdom of Losania. Providing Reito and the others with her country's lab facilities.

**Anastasia**

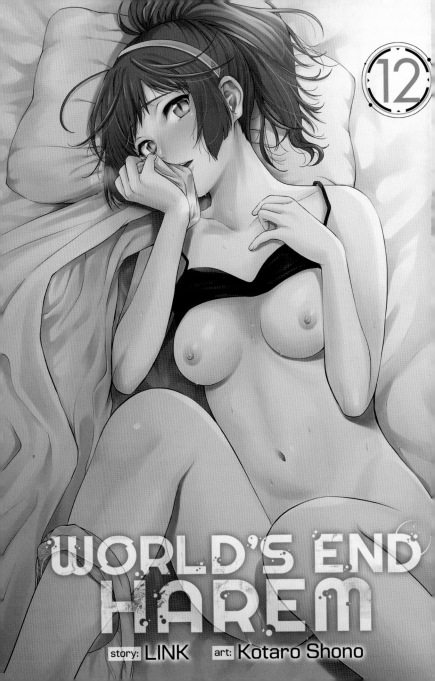

# WORLD'S END HAREM

story: LINK    art: Kotaro Shono